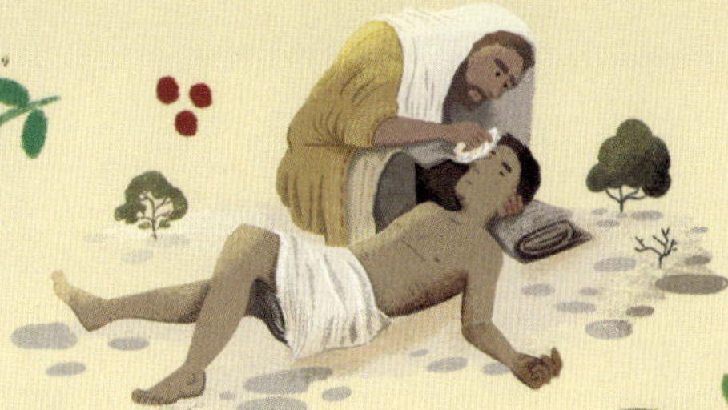

PRESENTED TO:

....

FROM:

....

DATE:

....

A Year of Bible Stories and Prayers

A Treasury of 96 Best-Loved Stories from God's Word

Print ISBN 979-8-89151-165-1

Published by Barbour Publishing, Inc., 1810 Barbour Drive, Uhrichsville, Ohio 44683,
www.barbourbooks.com

Our mission is to inspire the world with the life-changing message of the Bible.

Member of the Evangelical Christian Publishers Association

Printed in China.

002601 0825 HA

A Year of Bible Stories and Prayers

A Treasury of 96 Best-Loved Stories from God's Word

BARBOUR kidz
A Division of Barbour Publishing

written by JoAnne Simmons
illustrated by Anni Schmidt

CONTENTS

JANUARY – Beginnings & Protection

In the Beginning ... 14
The Story of Creation

The Great Flood ... 16
The Story of Noah

From Tragedy to Blessing ... 18
The Story of Job

The Road to Damascus ... 20
The Story of Paul

"This Nation Is Your People" ... 24
Moses' Prayer for God's Presence to Go with Israel to Canaan

"Lord, Save Me!" ... 26
Peter's Prayer to Be Saved from Drowning

"Open His Eyes, That He Might See" ... 28
Elisha's Prayer for His Servant's Understanding

"Not What I Want but What You Want" ... 30
Jesus' Prayer to Avoid the Suffering of the Cross

FEBRUARY – Love & Blessings

Loving Others Well ... 36
The Story of the Good Samaritan

A Deep and Lasting Friendship ... 38
The Story of David and Jonathan

Where You Go, I Will Go ... 40
The Story of Ruth

Love Changes a Heart ... 42
The Story of Zacchaeus

"Let Her Be the One" ... 46
Eliezer's Prayer to Find a Wife for Isaac

"Keep Them in the Power of Your Name" ... 48
Jesus' Prayer for His Followers

"Remember Me for This, God" ... 50
Nehemiah's Prayer for Blessing

"Well in Every Way" ... 52
John's Prayer That Gaius Would Prosper

MARCH – Easter & Healing

A Wonderful Invitation ... 58
The Story of the Last Supper

The Greatest Story of All Time ... 60
The Story of the Cross

An Empty Tomb ... 62
The Story of Jesus' Resurrection (Part 1)

He Lives! ... 64
The Story of Jesus' Resurrection (Part 2)

"Take Pity on Us, Son of David" ... 68
Two Men's Prayer for Healing from Blindness

"Please Put Your Hand on Him" ... 70
A Prayer for a Man Who Couldn't Hear or Speak

"Lord, You Can Heal Me!" ... 72
A Man's Prayer for Healing from Leprosy

"O God, Heal Her, I Pray!" ... 74
Moses' Prayer for Miriam

APRIL - Spring & Resurrection

An Epic Trust in God 80
The Story of Gideon

For Such a Time as This.......... 82
The Story of Esther

A Great Sacrifice.......... 84
The Story of Abraham and Isaac

One Thing That's Needed 86
The Story of Mary and Martha

"Father, I Thank You for Hearing Me" 90
Jesus' Prayer for the Resurrection of Lazarus

"Get Up, Tabitha!" 92
Peter's Prayer for Tabitha's Resurrection

"Let This Child's Life Return to Him" 94
Elijah's Prayer for the Resurrection of the Widow's Son

"Lord, Remember How I Have Walked with You" 96
Hezekiah's Prayer for a Longer Life

MAY - Celebration of Mothers

A Persistent Prayer 102
The Story of Hannah

Baby in a Basket.......... 104
The Story of Jochebed

Unlikely Mother.......... 106
The Story of Elizabeth

A Loving Mother-in-Law 108
The Story of Naomi

"Don't Forget Me!" 112
Hannah's Prayer for a Son

"My Heart Is Happy in the Lord!".......... 114
Hannah's Prayer of Gratitude

"Take Pity on Me, Lord" 116
A Mother's Prayer for Her Daughter

"Say That My Two Sons May Sit with You".......... 118
Salome's Prayer for Her Sons

JUNE - Celebration of Fathers

Jesus' Earthly Father.......... 124
The Story of Joseph

Father of the Wilderness Preacher.......... 126
The Story of Zechariah

Father of Twins 128
The Story of Isaac

A Plea for a Son's Healing.......... 130
The Story of the Nobleman

"Put Your Hand on Her That She May Be Healed".......... 134
Jairus' Prayer for His Daughter

"Lord, Have Pity on My Son!" 136
A Father's Prayer for His Demon-Possessed Boy

"Please Come to Capernaum!" 138
The Royal Official's Prayer for His Dying Son

"Lord, What Will You Give Me? For I Have No Child" 140
Abraham's Prayer for an Heir

JULY - Freedom & Forgiveness

The Lions' Den 146
The Story of Daniel

The Parting of the Red Sea 148
The Story of Moses

A Jailer Is Saved 150
The Story of Paul and Silas

The Courageous Dreamer 152
The Story of Joseph

"Take Away the Snakes" 156
Moses' Prayer for Forgiveness for the Israelites

"O Lord, Hear! O Lord, Forgive!" 158
Daniel's Prayer for Forgiveness of Israel's Sins

"Father, Forgive Them!" 160
Jesus' Prayer for the People Crucifying Him

"Lord, Do Not Hold This Sin Against Them" 162
Stephen's Prayer for His Killers

AUGUST - Learning and Wisdom & Victory in Battle

A Prayer for Wisdom 168
The Story of Solomon

When God Says, "Go" 170
The Story of Jonah

The Wife of a Very Foolish Man 172
The Story of Abigail

Spies in the Land 174
The Story of Joshua and Caleb

"Sun and Moon, Stand Still!" 178
Joshua's Prayer for a Miracle

"Give Me Strength Once More!" 180
Samson's Prayer to Defeat the Philistines

"Answer Me So These People May Know That You Are God!" 182
Elijah's Prayer for Fire from Heaven

"Lord, There Is No One but You to Help in the Battle!" 184
Asa's Prayer for Victory

SEPTEMBER - Strength and Perseverance & Silly Prayers

Only a Shepherd Boy 190
The Story of David

A Blazing Fiery Furnace 192
The Story of Shadrach, Meshach, and Abednego

From Death to Life 194
The Story of Lazarus

A Strongman's Secret 196
The Story of Samson

"O Lord God, for Sure You Have Fooled These People!" 200
Jeremiah's Prayer Accusing God

"No, I Could Never Do That, God!" 202
Ezekiel's Prayer of Protest

"O Lord, Why Have You Hurt These People?" 204
Moses' Prayer of Complaint to God

"God, I Thank You That I Am Not Like Other Men" 206
The Pharisee's Prideful Prayer

OCTOBER - Harvest & Wisdom

Overflowing Nets ... 212
The Story of the Fishers of Men

Five Loaves and Two Fish ... 214
The Story of the Feeding of the Five Thousand

Remembering God's Word ... 216
The Story of the Sower and the Seeds

The Scarlet Rope ... 218
The Story of Rahab

"Lord, You Know the Hearts of All Men" ... 222
The Disciples' Prayer for Wisdom in Replacing Judas

"Give Me an Understanding Heart" ... 224
Solomon's Prayer for Wisdom

"Show Me Something to Prove That It Is You Who Speaks with Me" ... 226
Gideon's Prayer for God's Assurance and Direction

"May the Lord Choose Someone Who Will Lead Them" ... 228
Moses' Prayer for a New Leader of Israel

NOVEMBER - Thanksgiving & Helpless Prayers

All She Had ... 234
The Story of the Widow Who Gave Two Mites

Living Water ... 236
The Story of the Woman at the Well

God Makes a Promise ... 238
The Story of Abraham and Sarah

Lost and Found! ... 240
The Story of the Prodigal Son

"You Have Brought Me Up from the Pit, God!" ... 244
Jonah's Prayer from Inside the Big Fish

"We Only Have Five Loaves of Bread and Two Fish!" ... 246
The Disciples' Prayer for Jesus to Help Feed the People

"The Burden Is Too Much" ... 248
Moses' Prayer for Relief

"My God, Why Have You Left Me Alone?" ... 250
Jesus' Prayer on the Cross

DECEMBER - Christmas & Prayers By and About Jesus

A Heavenly Greeting ... 256
The Story of Mary, Mother of Jesus

Another Miraculous Birth ... 258
The Story of John the Baptist

Birth of a King ... 260
The Story of Baby Jesus

The Rising Star ... 262
The Story of the Wise Men

"My Eyes Have Seen the Chosen One" ... 266
Simeon's Prayer About Jesus

"Our Father in Heaven, Your Name is Holy" ... 268
Jesus' Teaching About How to Pray

"Father, Honor Your Name!" ... 270
Jesus' Prayer for God's Glory

"I Thank You, Father" ... 272
Jesus' Prayer of Gratitude

JANUARY

Beginnings

If you've ever heard the stories of creation and Noah's ark, and if you know all about the lives of Paul and Job, you might wonder what these four Bible stories have in common. God created the earth and everything in it—including the very first man and woman, Adam and Eve; Noah built a massive ark that saved him and his family from a wild flood; Saul (who was also called Paul) experienced quite an adventure on the road to Damascus (he was even blind for a time!); and Job had everything a person could ever want or need, and then he lost it all—but *still* he was greatly blessed. While each of these Bible stories is quite different, each shares a message of new beginnings.

A new beginning is wonderful. It's a fresh start. Think about your worst day ever. . . then think about how you felt once that day was done and you had the promise of a brand-new day ahead. Pretty great, right? God, who is overflowing with love and grace (grace is when you get something awesome that you don't deserve), allows new beginnings all the time. He allowed do-overs for the people we read about in His Word, the Bible. And He allows do-overs for us today.

What's so special about new beginnings? Read the following stories and see for yourself!

IN THE BEGINNING

The Story of Creation

Imagine the very first new beginning. What was it like when God created the earth and everything in it—out of nothing? Absolutely *nothing*? It's incredible to think about everything He made!

At first, there were no people on the earth. There were no animals on the earth. There were no flowers to pick or trees to climb or mud puddles to jump into on the earth. There was no light to see a thing on the earth. Not a thing! There was not even any shape to the earth. There simply was no earth.

There was only God. And when He spoke, He could make anything come to be. So that's exactly what He did.

He said, "Let there be light." And there was light. He called the light "day" and the darkness "night." That was the very first day.

He said, "Let there be space between the heavens and the earth." He called that space the "sky." That was the second day.

He said, "Let there be land and seas and plants and trees." And He formed the earth with land and sea and plants and trees. That was the third day.

He said, "Let there be sun and moon and stars." And there were sun and moon and stars. That was the fourth day.

He said, "Let there be all kinds of swimming creatures and all kinds of flying creatures." And there were all kinds of fish to fill the waters and all kinds of birds to fill the skies. That was the fifth day.

He said, "Let there be all kinds of land animals—cuddly ones and crawling ones and slithering ones and wild ones." And there were all kinds of animals to fill the land. Then He said, "Let there be people, made a lot like Me. Let them rule over all the fish and birds and land animals." And there were people made to rule over all the creatures of the earth. That was the sixth day.

God saw everything He made, and He saw that it was good. On the seventh day, God rested, and He blessed the seventh day and made it an extra special day, a holy day.

These were the very first days, which made up the very first week. God created the earth and everything in it brand-new. This was the beginning of all new beginnings!

(Adapted from Genesis 1:1–2:3)

THE GREAT FLOOD

The Story of Noah

God had a wonderful plan for His brand-new, beautiful creation. He told the first people, Adam and Eve, to have a great big family to start filling up the world with many more people. But Adam and Eve also started filling up the world with something else. Something very bad. Something called sin.

Sin is choosing to disobey God's rules. These are good rules meant to help people and let them be close to God. After Adam and Eve made the world's first bad choice, sin suddenly touched everything everywhere. And it just wouldn't stop. As more people filled the earth, more sin spread among them. Years upon years passed. Many people lived. Sin upon sin increased.

One day God said, "I've had enough." He was angry, troubled, and sad over people choosing to be wicked instead of choosing to follow Him. So He planned a new beginning and shared it with one good man who still followed Him—Noah.

God told Noah He was going to send a huge flood to wash away wickedness in the world. And then Noah and his wife and their children could start brand-new. He instructed Noah to build a great big boat, called an ark, that would save Noah and his family from the coming flood. Then Noah obeyed God by bringing two of every kind of animal on board the ark. Two sheep. . .two cows. . .two rabbits. . .two owls. On and on, two by two, creatures filled up that big ark like a zoo! Finally, God closed the ark's doors and sent the rain pouring and the floodwaters rising.

For forty days and forty nights the rain came down and the waters rose up.

Eventually, water covered even the highest mountaintops. The flood drowned and destroyed everything on the earth. *Everything.* But the ark God designed floated safely above it all. God protected Noah and his family and the many animals.

Finally, God pushed all the floodwaters away and set the ark on dry land. He called Noah and his family and the animals out of the ark and told them, "Live and love and fill the earth brand-new!" He gave a brand-new promise too. God said that He would never destroy all life on earth with water again. Then He painted colors in the sky—a rainbow!—to represent that promise. Every rainbow ever since has shown that God is a keeper of His promises and the giver of new beginnings. And every rainbow always will.

(Adapted from Genesis 6–9)

FROM TRAGEDY TO BLESSING

The Story of Job

Many years after Noah lived, a man named Job lived in a land called Uz. Like Noah, Job was a very good man who loved and followed God. He had a wife and a large family, with seven sons and three daughters. Job loved them all dearly and cared for them well. His faith was great; he wanted nothing to do with wickedness. And he was very wealthy too. He owned seven thousand sheep, three thousand camels, five hundred pair of oxen, and five hundred donkeys. Job also had many servants working for him. No wonder he was called the greatest man among all the people of the East!

But sometimes awful things happen to good people. And awful things happened to Job. Job lost all his children on the same day and all his animals and wealth too. Oh, how sad Job was. Yet, even with a broken heart, Job still loved and worshipped and followed God. He said, "The Lord gave and the Lord has taken away. Praise the name of the Lord" (Job 1:21 NLV).

Surely Job couldn't handle another hard thing. But next, he caught a terrible disease—nasty sores on his skin from head to toe. Yet, even in pain and suffering, Job still loved and praised and followed God—at first. Soon Job grew too weary of his suffering. He was tired and hurting and angry.

He cried out to God in pain and confusion. Job blamed God for all that was wrong. Job needed a new beginning.

So, out of a strong and stormy wind, God spoke sternly to Job to remind him of His great power and His amazing goodness. God spoke sternly to Job to help him see he needed to be sorry for the way he had blamed God. And then Job did see, and he was sorry and sad for his sin. He prayed for forgiveness, and God listened and forgave Job. Then God restored to Job all he had lost—plus much, much more!

In joy and in pain, in plenty and in loss, in tragedy and in blessing, God loved Job and never left him. Job's story reminds us that, in all things—good or bad—God is working and making a way for new beginnings.

(Adapted from the book of Job)

THE ROAD TO DAMASCUS

The Story of Paul

Many, many years after Noah and Job lived, there was a man named Saul who was very different from Noah and Job. He was not a good man. He pretended to love God, but he hated people who believed in Jesus Christ, the Son of God. He hated these followers of Christ so much he hunted them down to capture them, put them in chains, beat them, and kill them. Saul was an awful, violent man.

One day, Saul was traveling to a city called Damascus, and God gave Saul a new beginning. God made a bright light flash around Saul to stop him on the road. Saul dropped to the ground as a voice called out to him, "Saul, why are you working so cruelly against Me?"

"Who are you?" Saul asked.

"I am Jesus, the one you are hurting," the voice said. "Now get up and go into the city, and someone there will tell you what to do next."

But when Saul got up, he couldn't see! The men traveling with him had to lead him into the city. For three days Saul was blind and would not eat or drink.

Meanwhile God spoke to a man named Ananias and told him to help bring about Saul's new beginning. Ananias was a little nervous about going to a scary man like Saul. He'd heard how Saul captured and killed people. Surely God didn't want Ananias to help such a dangerous guy! But God reassured Ananias that He had important work for Saul to do and all would be fine. So Ananias obeyed. He found Saul exactly where God said he would be.

Ananias put his hands on Saul and said, "Jesus sent me to you. He stopped you on the road with the great light. He sent me so you can see again and be filled with God's Holy Spirit." Right then something scaly fell off Saul's eyes, and he was no longer blind. He got up and was baptized, and then he spent time with followers of Jesus. Soon he was preaching, "Jesus is the Son of God!"

All the people who heard Saul were amazed by the change in him. They could hardly believe the difference. God filled Saul with His power so Saul could preach that Jesus is the Son of God. Saul was also known by the name Paul, and from then on, he no longer captured and killed Christians; instead, he helped people *become* Christians! Paul continued to do many great things for God, all because of his new beginning.

(Adapted from Acts 9:1–31)

Prayers for Protection

The world is full of good things that give us fun and joy and giggles. The world also has some sad and scary things that make us worry and cry and feel afraid. But above all of these things stands our great big God. Can you picture Him? He's watching over you with love every moment of every day, in the good times and the bad. He knows, He cares, He provides, and He protects—not always the way you want or expect Him to, but always in the ways that are best. Throughout the Bible, we see time and again how people prayed to God for help and protection from the sad and scary things of life. These examples help us remember to pray for God's help and protection too. Read the following stories and see for yourself!

"THIS NATION IS YOUR PEOPLE"

Moses' Prayer for God's Presence to Go with Israel to Canaan

Back in ancient Bible times, the baby who floated down the Nile River in a basket grew up to be the man God chose to lead His people, the Israelites, out of slavery in Egypt. That man was Moses, and God talked to Moses just like a friend.

God instructed Moses to lead the people for forty years in the wilderness as He worked out His good plans for them. He showed them miraculous things like parting the Red Sea so they could walk right through. He used a pillar of cloud to lead them during the day and a pillar of fire to lead them by night. He gave them meat to eat each night. And He gave them bread, called manna, which rained down from heaven every morning. But even as God took such good care of them, sometimes the Israelites didn't like what God was doing and the places where He was leading. Sometimes they grumbled and complained. They were impatient and rude and made bad choices. They even melted down all their golden earrings to create a false god to worship instead of the one true God.

That was a big mistake, and God became very angry—angry enough that He told them He would no longer be with them to help them and protect them. But God's anger never kept Him from loving them. He still let Moses talk to Him on their behalf. Moses pleaded with God not to leave the Israelites alone. He said, "This nation is Your people. Don't let us leave this place without You." Moses knew they would all be lost and in great danger if God was not with them. The people needed God to be present in their lives to guide and protect them.

God was pleased with Moses. He listened with compassion to Moses' prayer for help, and He answered, "I Myself will go with you. I will give you rest." God loves His people no matter what, and God hears and answers honest, humble prayers for His help and His presence and His protection.

(Adapted from Exodus 2; 13–14; 31–33)

"LORD, SAVE ME!"

Peter's Prayer to Be Saved from Drowning

Jesus loved His friends, the disciples, and He loved all the people who came to Him to learn and to be healed. But sometimes He needed quiet time alone to rest and pray to God the Father.

One day, after His miracle of turning five small loaves of bread and two fish into a lunch big enough to feed more than five thousand people, Jesus told His disciples to get in their boat and go on ahead. He was headed up the mountain alone for time to talk to God the Father.

Later that night, the disciples in the boat found themselves tossed around in the middle of a storm. The wind and the waves were strong and wild. And just before dawn, they looked out on the water and froze, suddenly very afraid. "It's a ghost!" they cried.

But it wasn't a ghost at all. It was Jesus! "Don't be afraid," He told them. "It's Me!"

Jesus' friend Peter was very bold and brave, and he loved Jesus very much. He said, "Lord, if it's You, tell me to walk out to You on the water."

And Jesus said, "Come on, then!"

So Peter got out of the boat and took one step—and then another! He was walking on water just like Jesus!

Before long, though, Peter noticed the strong wind. He surely felt those wild waves. He grew very afraid, and he started to sink. "Lord, save me!" he cried out to Jesus.

And right away, Jesus grabbed Peter by the hand, and Peter was safe.

Jesus said to Peter, "You have so little faith! Why did you doubt?"

Then Jesus and Peter got into the boat, and the storm quickly stopped.

Everyone in the boat worshipped Jesus and told Him, "You are the Son of God!"

Jesus loves when people are full of strong faith and courage, yet He knows that sometimes our faith and courage grow weak. But when people cry out to Him, "Lord, save me!" He reaches out to answer that prayer with great big love and exactly the help that we need.

(Adapted from Matthew 14)

"OPEN HIS EYES, THAT HE MIGHT SEE"

Elisha's Prayer for His Servant's Understanding

When the nation of Syria was fighting against God's nation of Israel, the prophet Elisha, who spoke for God, was helping the Israelites and warning them of danger. God gave Elisha the power to know what the Syrian king was saying and the moves he would make. So Elisha helped protect the Israelites by telling them where to go to avoid being killed and defeated in battle.

The king of Syria was very angry because of this. He called his servants and said to them, "Show me which one of us is helping the king of Israel!" He thought there must be a traitor among them.

But one of his men told him about Elisha being a prophet of God. "None of us is a traitor, O king," the man said. "Elisha tells the king of Israel the very words you say in your bedroom."

So the king of Syria said, "Go and see where Elisha is." And he soon sent an army of many soldiers to find and capture the man of God. They snuck in at night and gathered around the city where Elisha was staying.

Early in the morning Elisha's servant went out and saw the enemy army ready to capture Elisha. "This is really bad!" he told Elisha. "What should we do?"

"Don't be afraid," Elisha said to his servant, "for those who are with us are more than those who are with them." And then he prayed, "O Lord, open his eyes, that he might see."

And God opened the eyes of Elisha's servant and showed him that the mountain around them was full of horses and chariots of fire. They were ready to protect and fight for God's people of Israel!

Then Elisha prayed that the enemy army would be blinded so that he could lead them unaware to another city—right where the armies of Israel could capture them. And when God opened their eyes again, they realized where they were. But Elisha told the king of Israel to be kind to them. So the king fed them a meal and sent them away.

God's people today might often feel outnumbered by enemies, but we can call on Him—anytime, anywhere—to open our eyes so that we might see the miraculous ways He loves us and fights for us and protects us.

(Adapted from 2 Kings 6)

"NOT WHAT I WANT BUT WHAT YOU WANT"

Jesus' Prayer to Avoid the Suffering of the Cross

When the time was drawing near for Jesus to suffer and die on the cross, He needed to pray to God the Father. He went to a garden called Gethsemane with three of His disciples. He said to them, "My soul is very sad. Please stay here with Me, keep watch with Me, and pray with Me."

Then He went a little farther into the garden and got down with His face on the ground. He prayed to ask God the Father—if there was any way to do it—to please protect Him and take away the suffering that He knew was about to happen with His death on the cross. "But," He added, "not what I want but what You want."

Then He went back to His three friends and found that they were asleep. That upset Him. "Couldn't you watch and pray with Me for just one hour?" He asked them. He needed encouragement, but His friends had let Him down. So He asked them again to watch and pray—and stay awake this time!

Again He went alone to pray to God, saying, "My Father, if this must happen to Me, may whatever You want be done." And then He went back to His friends and found them sleeping again. So He went away from them a third time and prayed to God the same prayer—"Not what I want but what You want."

Finally, Jesus went back to His sleepy friends and told them to get up because it would soon be time for God's plans for Him to unfold. The Father's will would be done.

Jesus is our perfect hero and example. We can pray for protection from suffering, just like He did. But even more importantly, just like Jesus, we should pray for what God wants to be done—even if it's very different from what we want. Through Jesus' suffering and death and rising to life again, God was working to save people. And in whatever suffering we must go through, God is working out His perfect plans too.

(Adapted from Matthew 26)

FEBRUARY

Love

Red and pink and hearts and candy. Is that what love is? Or hugs and kisses and warm fuzzy snuggles. Is that what love is? Or dating and romance and big fancy weddings. Is that what love is? The answer is this: if God is in them, yes! Everything we know about real love comes from God. He is love, the Bible tells us (1 John 4:16). "We know what love is because Jesus gave his life for us" (1 John 3:16 CEV); and "God showed how much he loved us by having Christ die for us, even though we were sinful" (Romans 5:8 CEV).

So if we truly know God and obey Him according to His Word, any act of love with God as the source is real love. If you color a valentine to encourage a friend and you do it with God's love in your heart, that is real love. If you surprise your mom with the tightest of hugs for no reason at all and you do it with God's love in your heart, that is real love. If you patiently help your little brother tie his shoes and you do it with God's love in your heart, that is real love. If a man and woman date and get married with God's love in their hearts, that is real love.

Throughout all of His Word, God teaches us and shows us examples of His real love. Read the following stories and see for yourself!

LOVING OTHERS WELL

The Story of the Good Samaritan

One day back in Bible times, a religious expert asked Jesus what he needed to do to have his life last forever. Jesus helped him remember that the Bible says to love the Lord your God with all your heart, all your soul, all your strength, and all your mind, and to love your neighbor as you love yourself. And Jesus said, "Do this and you will have life."

The religious expert replied by asking, "Well, who is my neighbor?"

So Jesus shared a story to help the man learn. Jesus' story was about a Jewish man who was traveling from a place called Jerusalem to a place called Jericho. But along the way, the Jewish man was attacked by robbers. The nasty robbers stole everything from the man, even his clothes. Then they beat him and left him to die on the side of the road.

Soon a religious leader called a priest came by on the same road. *Surely* the priest would help the poor Jewish man who'd been left to die alongside the road. But the religious leader did not help! He saw the poor man, but he walked right past on the other side of the road.

Next, a man from the family of Levi passed by. Surely *he* would help the poor Jewish man who'd been left to die alongside the road. But the Levite did not help either! He saw the poor man, but he walked right past on the other side of the road.

Finally a man called a Samaritan—who normally would have had *nothing* to do with a Jewish man because there was great hatred among Jews and Samaritans—saw the poor Jewish man lying alongside the road. The Samaritan felt sorry for the Jewish man. With compassion, the Samaritan went to the man and cared for his wounds and

bandaged him up. Then the Samaritan helped the injured man onto a donkey, took him to an inn, and paid for him to have a safe place to rest and get well.

When Jesus was done sharing this story, He asked the religious expert, "Which of the three men was a neighbor to the man who was attacked by the robbers?"

And the religious leader said, "The one who helped."

And Jesus said, "That's right. Now go and do the same kind of thing."

With total love for God in heart and soul and strength and mind, a person who helps others—no matter who they are—is a person who knows and shows what real love is.

(Adapted from Luke 10:25–37)

A DEEP AND LASTING FRIENDSHIP

The Story of David and Jonathan

After David bravely killed the giant Goliath, Saul, who was king of Israel, was greatly impressed. So King Saul called David to come and talk to him, and David soon met the king's son Jonathan. In no time, there was an extraspecial bond between the two young men. Jonathan loved David and made him a promise to be a loyal friend forever.

Since David was such a brave young man, King Saul wanted David to work for him and lead his armies. And because God was with him, David succeeded in all he did. But then one day King Saul grew jealous that maybe the people of Israel respected David more than they respected him. The king grew *so* jealous that he no longer trusted David, and he actually wanted to kill David! He told all his servants and even his son Jonathan to kill David.

Never could Jonathan kill his best friend David. Instead, he warned David about the king's orders. Jonathan helped protect David. Then he defended David by reminding his father, "David has never done any wrong to you. He has only helped you! Remember how he killed Goliath? God won a great victory for Israel through David that day. You saw it and were glad. So why would you now want to kill David, an innocent man, for no reason at all?" Jonathan convinced King Saul to trust David again.

But it didn't take long for King Saul to once again grow jealous and think evil thoughts toward David. He attacked David. And Jonathan again helped protect his good friend from his father's evil plans. Jonathan encouraged and loved David. Jonathan said to his friend, "Whatever you want me to do, I'll do for you." And he stayed true to that promise. He risked his own life to protect and help David in every way he could, despite the anger of King Saul. Jonathan knew his father's plans were wrong, and he would stay loyal to David no matter what.

Jonathan could have become jealous of David. He could have wanted to become the next king after Saul instead of David. But Jonathan loved God and loved his friend David—with the real kind of love that cares for others more than self, the real kind of love that is loyal and true.

(Adapted from 1 Samuel 18–20)

WHERE YOU GO, I WILL GO

The Story of Ruth

In a land called Moab, there lived a young woman named Ruth. She married a man who had traveled from Bethlehem to settle in Moab. He had traveled with his parents and his brother. The four had left Bethlehem because there was great famine—barely anything to eat!—in the land there.

About ten years after Ruth married her husband, he died. Ruth's brother-in-law also died. And her father-in-law had already died too. So, of the family, only Ruth, her mother-in-law named Naomi, and her sister-in-law named Orpah were left. They were in a terribly sad situation. Surely they missed their husbands, and in those days, to be a woman without a man to take care of her was very difficult indeed. It was hard for women alone to find good work, enough food, and a safe place to live.

Naomi told Ruth and Orpah to leave her and go back to their old homes since they were still young. They could find new husbands. At first they wouldn't think of it. They wanted to stay with Naomi and go with her to her people.

But Naomi said to them, "Why would you come with me? I am too old to have another husband."

Orpah finally decided to leave and kissed her mother-in-law goodbye.

But Ruth refused. She clung to Naomi, saying, "Please don't push me to leave you! I want to go where you go. I want to stay where you stay. I want your people to be my people. I want your God to be my God. I never want to leave you as long as I am alive."

When Naomi realized Ruth's great and loyal love for her, she stopped pushing her to go. The older woman and the younger woman traveled together back to Bethlehem. They had heard that God had helped His people by ending the famine there.

In Bethlehem, God blessed Ruth as she worked in fields to pick up leftover grain. God led her to the fields owned by a kind and good man named Boaz. When Boaz heard about Ruth's loyalty and love for her mother-in-law, he was impressed, and he admired her. He protected and provided for Ruth and Naomi and grew to love Ruth.

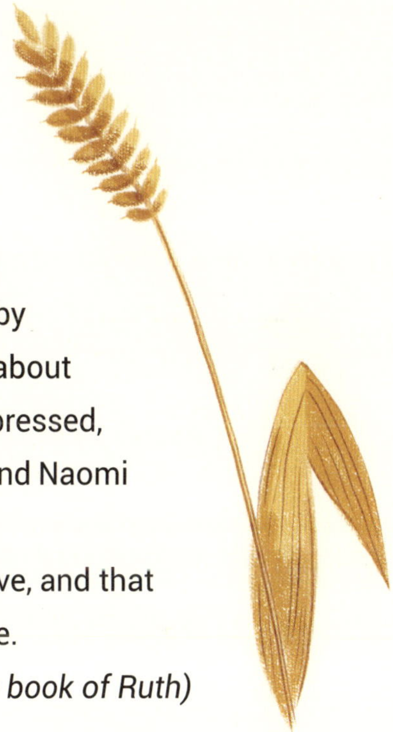

Ruth loved Naomi with a real, never-leaving kind of love, and that great love inspired blessings and *more* never-leaving love.

(Adapted from the book of Ruth)

LOVE CHANGES A HEART

The Story of Zacchaeus

Zacchaeus was a man who lived in Jesus' time. He was a tax collector in the city of Jericho—a chief tax collector, and he was very wealthy. Men like him were known for being terribly unfair. They cheated and took far too much of other people's money. So most people in Jericho hated and avoided Zacchaeus.

But Zacchaeus was drawn to Jesus. He wanted to see Jesus as He traveled through Jericho. Even though Zacchaeus was not very tall and it would be hard for him to find a good view among the crowds of people, he was determined. He ran ahead of where Jesus would walk, and he climbed a big tree, a sycamore tree! High in the branches, he waited and watched for the one called the Son of God.

Soon Jesus was traveling by! And when He reached that sycamore tree, He stopped. He looked up. He spotted Zacchaeus. Then He called him by name and said, "Come down right away. I am going to your house today."

Zacchaeus was totally amazed and so excited! He happily climbed down at once and welcomed Jesus to his home.

Meanwhile, most people of Jericho were shocked, and they complained. How could this be? Why would Jesus *ever* go to the home of a bad man like Zacchaeus?

But as Zacchaeus spent time with Jesus, he was sorry for his sins. He wanted to make all his wrongs right. He wanted to help the poor. He wanted to give back all the money he had cheated, plus four times more!

And Jesus said to Zacchaeus, "Today salvation has come to you." He explained how He had come to look for and save those who were stuck in sin, those who were lost—those like Zacchaeus.

To love someone who is kind and good is not usually hard. But to love someone who is selfish and unfair is very, very hard. But Jesus loved Zacchaeus and saved him from his sin. Jesus changed his life and his heart. Jesus showed the example of real and perfect love.

(Adapted from Luke 19:1–10)

Prayers of Love and Blessing

February makes us think of Valentine's Day, and Valentine's Day makes us think of love! And love should make us think of God because if not for Him, we wouldn't know how to love at all. He created love. The Bible says God *is* love. Think of the people who love and bless you in your life, like your mom or dad, grandpa or grandma, brother or sister, and your favorite teachers, coaches, and babysitters. The Bible says if those people know how wonderful it is to love you and give you good blessings, then you should think of how much more God, your heavenly Father who created you, must want to love and bless you. It's oodles and *oodles* more! As you are filled with love and blessings from the people who love you and the one true God who loves you, you should want that love and blessing to overflow out of you and onto others. Do you pray for love and blessings for others? People in Bible times did. Jesus did too. And we can learn from them. Read the following stories and see for yourself!

"LET HER BE THE ONE"

Eliezer's Prayer to Find a Wife for Isaac

Isaac was the son born to Abraham and Sarah after they thought they were far too old to have children. But God promised they would have a son, and God's promises are always true. One day, after Isaac was all grown up, Abraham said to his servant Eliezer, "Go to my home country, and the people I grew up with, to find a bride for Isaac."

But Eliezer had a question. "What if the woman doesn't want to follow me back here to this land? Shouldn't I take your son with me to the land where you came from?"

Abraham insisted he should not. "God promised me: 'I will give this land to your children and to their children's children.' He will send His angel in front of you to help make sure you can find a bride for my son from there."

So Eliezer loaded ten camels with lots of supplies and lots of gifts, and he set off to a place called Nahor to find a bride for Isaac. It was a long journey, and by the time Eliezer and the ten camels finally arrived, they were tired. And hot. And very thirsty. They stopped outside the city near a well of water in the evening, and Eliezer let the camels get down on their knees to rest. Then he asked God to show him who should be Isaac's wife. He prayed, "O Lord, here by the well, I can watch the daughters of the men of the city come get water. If I say to a girl, 'Could you let me drink a little water from your jar, please?' and she answers, 'Drink, and I will give water to your camels also,' let her be the one You have chosen to be Isaac's wife." And before he had even finished praying, a beautiful young woman named Rebekah came out to the well with a water jar on her shoulder.

"Could you let me drink a little water from your jar, please?" Eliezer asked her.

"Yes," she said. "Drink." And she gave him her water jar. Then she said, "And I will get water for your camels also." And she did.

Eliezer thought, *She must be the one!* God had answered his prayer so quickly! He soon met Rebekah's family. He told them how he had prayed and how God answered that prayer through Rebekah when she gave both him and his camels water. He said, "I bowed low and worshipped. I gave honor and thanks to the Lord, the God of my boss, Abraham. For God led me in the right way."

And Rebekah's father and brother answered, "This is surely from the Lord. Take Rebekah to be the wife of your boss's son."

God was pleased that Eliezer wanted to bless Abraham by bringing home the right bride for Isaac. Eliezer's name means "God is my help," and God surely showed His help to Eliezer and His blessing to Abraham and Isaac through Rebekah.

(Adapted from Genesis 24)

"KEEP THEM IN THE POWER OF YOUR NAME"

Jesus' Prayer for His Followers

When Jesus lived on earth, He traveled and taught and preached. He made friends and enemies. He camped under the stars. He walked on water and calmed stormy seas. He healed people who were blind and deaf and sick. He brought dead people back to life. He turned a little bit of food into a great big picnic lunch! And He blessed and loved and cared for all the people. On top of these many things, Jesus prayed for people too.

One day after He had been preaching and teaching, He began to pray for His friends, the disciples. Jesus prayed to His Father in heaven, saying, "I have made Your name known to My friends. You gave them to Me. They have obeyed Your Word. Now they know that everything You have given Me came from You. I gave them the Word, and they received it. They know I came from You, and they believe You sent Me."

Then He prayed for God to bless His friends and keep them in the power of God's name after Jesus joined His Father in heaven. "I am coming to You," He prayed, "but these friends are still in the world. Holy Father, keep them in the power of Your name. Then they will be one, even as We are one."

And finally, He prayed for His disciples, saying, "Keep them from the devil. My followers do not belong to the world, just as I do not belong to the world. Make them holy by Your Word, which is truth. You sent Me into the world, and I have sent them into the world."

And then Jesus prayed for all His friends and followers in the future too—including me, including you! He said, "I pray for those who will put their trust in Me through the teaching they have heard. May they be united, Father, just like You are in Me and I am in You. May they belong to Us. Then the world will believe that You sent Me and that You love them as You love Me."

(Adapted from John 17)

"REMEMBER ME FOR THIS, GOD"

Nehemiah's Prayer for Blessing

Nehemiah was a Jewish man who lived in ancient Bible times. He served as the cupbearer for the king of Persia. Cupbearers had a serious job—the job of tasting all the king's food and drink before the king did. That way, the cupbearer could make sure no one was trying to poison the king!

One day Nehemiah looked sad, and the king noticed. He said, "Why is your face so sad when you are not sick, Nehemiah? Are you sad in your heart?"

Nehemiah replied, "How can my face not be sad when my family's city is in ruins?"

So the king said, "What is it you are asking for?"

Nehemiah replied, "If it pleases you, and if you approve, send me to Jerusalem. Let me build the city again."

The king liked Nehemiah and had been pleased with his work, so he gave Nehemiah permission to go. Nehemiah soon got a group of good builders together, and within fifty-two days, they rebuilt the city of Jerusalem's walls! It was a great big job in a short amount of time, and it showed God's great big power was at work in His people. Nehemiah loved and respected God with all his heart, and he continued to help the Jewish people honor and obey God in all things.

At the end of his life, Nehemiah thought back over the good deeds he had done—the ways he helped the Jewish people follow God. He said, "I went to Jerusalem and learned about the sinful things done to the house of God. I was very angry. I said, 'Why is the house of God no longer cared for?' " Nehemiah had helped the people correct their wrongs, and he prayed, "Remember me for this, God. Do not forget the good works I have done for the house of my God and His worship."

And as he thought back over more good deeds from his life—like how he helped the Jewish people follow God's commands—he prayed again. "Remember me for this also, God. Be good to me because You are loving."

Nehemiah reminds us that our good deeds for God matter. When we love and serve Him faithfully and inspire others to follow His ways, we can ask God to remember what we have done and bless us too!

(Adapted from Nehemiah 1–6; 13)

"WELL IN EVERY WAY"

John's Prayer That Gaius Would Prosper

Jesus had twelve disciples, and two of them were brothers named James and John. Jesus called them the Sons of Thunder! They were bold and brave and eager as they followed Jesus and learned from Him. One day when the people of a town in Samaria did not want to welcome Jesus into the town, James and John asked Him, "Jesus, do You want us to call down fire from heaven to burn the town up?" Jesus had to settle them down.

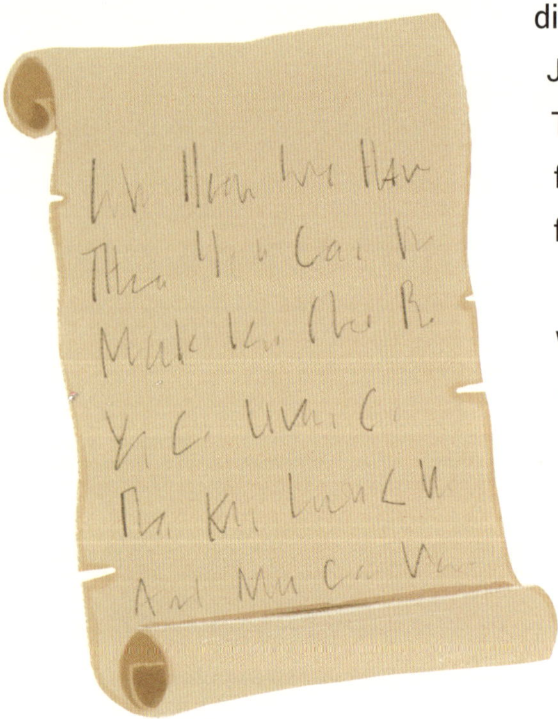

When Jesus was dying on the cross, John was the disciple He asked to look after His mother, Mary. Jesus said to Mary, "Woman, look at your son." Then He said to John, "Look at your mother." And from then on, Mary lived with John, and he cared for her as if she really was his mother.

Later in his life, John was a busy writer. He wrote five books of the Bible! He wrote the Gospel of John to describe the life and work of Jesus. He wrote the book of Revelation to record his visions about the last days of this world. And he wrote three letters called 1 John, 2 John, and 3 John.

In the first of these letters, John wrote to make sure the Christians then and the

Christians now would know that Jesus was a real man, and He was also really God—and that He loves people so much. In the second letter, John wrote to warn people against false teachers. And in the third letter, John wrote to his friend Gaius to encourage him to always do what is good and not do what is evil. Gaius was faithful to God and to others, and he was kind and welcoming to strangers. He was known for his love and for walking in truth.

John wrote to Gaius in his letter, "I love you, dear friend. I pray that you are doing well in every way. I pray that your body and soul are strong and well."

Who are the loved ones and friends you pray for like that? Whose body and soul do you want to be strong and well in every way? Pray blessings on them just like Jesus' friend John did for his friend Gaius!

(Adapted from Mark 3; Luke 9; John 19; 3 John)

MARCH

Easter

Think of your favorite stories and movies. Don't the best ones have a surprise somewhere? A twist you never expected and an ending you never imagined? God's greatest story is like that too. God's Word tells the story of how He created and loved and guided and saved His people, with lots of twists and turns and surprises. And the very best part is that it's all true! Even better—it's still coming true. The Bible is complete, but God's story and your story aren't over yet. He's working through His Word and His people, leading and saving and giving everlasting life to all who believe in His Son, Jesus Christ.

The story of Easter is the part of God's story when, in an unexpected way, God saved and offered eternal life to His people through Jesus. Read the following stories and see for yourself!

A WONDERFUL INVITATION

The Story of the Last Supper

When Jesus grew up to be a man, He began His ministry. He chose good friends—they were called His disciples. He traveled with them, and He taught, and He healed people. He said and proved He was the Son of God. As His ministry was ending, He wanted a last meal with His disciples, a special meal held at the time of a Jewish celebration feast called Passover.

When His friends asked, "Where do you want to have the Passover meal?" Jesus sent two of them into the city of Jerusalem with specific instructions. They were to meet up with a man carrying a jar of water who would take them to a house with a large room perfect for their feast.

The disciples did what Jesus instructed, and in the evening they sat down to eat the Passover meal. During this meal, Jesus shocked His disciples when He got up from eating, took off His outer robe, wrapped a towel around His waist, and knelt down to begin washing each of their dirty feet. In the disciples' minds that was something only a servant should do, never Jesus their Teacher and Lord!

But Jesus said, "Yes, I am your Teacher and Lord, and I'm teaching you by example. I have served you, and so you should serve one another. You will be blessed if you serve like I do."

And as they ate the meal, their Last Supper together, Jesus taught His disciples more about what was going to happen to Him, even though they didn't fully understand. He took bread and thanked God for it and broke it in pieces and gave it to the disciples. Then

He said, "This is My body, which is given for you. Do this to remember Me." He also took a cup of wine and thanked God for it. Then He gave it to them, and they all drank from it. Jesus said, "This is My blood that confirms the promise between God and His people. It is poured out so that the sins of many people can be forgiven."

At the Last Supper, Jesus gave His friends who were present and all friends in the future who would believe in Him an invitation. It was an invitation to be a humble servant like Him and be blessed; and it was also an invitation to believe, remember, and receive that His body and His blood were meant to be broken and poured out to save people from their sins.

Jesus' invitation is the most wonderful of all time.

(Adapted from Matthew 26:17–30; Mark 14:12–26; Luke 22:7–30; John 13:1–30)

THE GREATEST STORY OF ALL TIME

The Story of the Cross

The greatest story of all time is the saddest of all time—but only at first. Because Jesus suffered for things He didn't even do.

After Jesus shared the Last Supper with His disciples and predicted His death and the events that would surround it, all those things started to come true. One friend named Judas betrayed Jesus. He helped soldiers find and capture Jesus in exchange for thirty pieces of silver. Then those soldiers took Jesus to the Jewish leaders who were accusing Him of crimes. From there Jesus was led to the palace of Pilate, the Roman governor. Pilate did not believe in Jesus, but he did not think Jesus was a criminal, and Pilate did not want to kill Jesus. He handed Jesus over to let the Jewish people beat Him. They spit on Him and put a painful crown of thorns on His head. They mocked and taunted Him and hit Him in the face.

Pilate tried again to free Jesus, but the Jewish people kept shouting and persuading until Pilate gave up and gave in. And so the soldiers led Jesus to a place called Golgotha, where they nailed His hands and feet to a cross and raised Him up to suffer and die in front of all the people watching.

Two other men were being crucified next to Jesus. One of them said mean things to Jesus, but the other had faith and said to Jesus, "Remember me when You come into Your kingdom."

And Jesus promised him, "Today you will be with Me in paradise."

At noon, darkness fell across the land—in the middle of the day! At three o'clock, Jesus

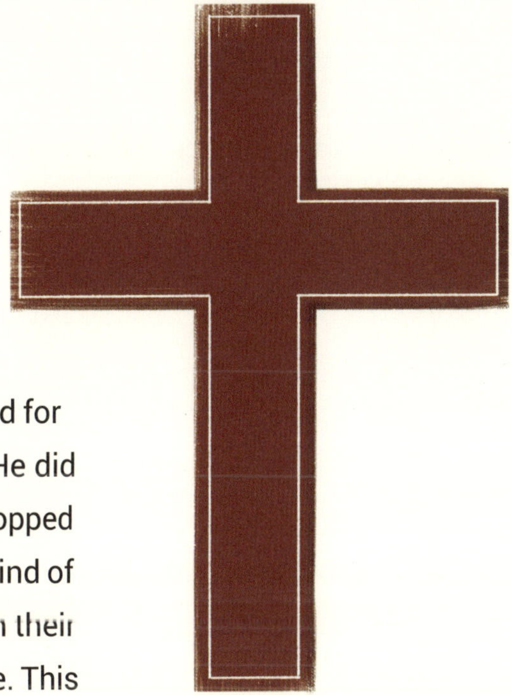

cried out to God, "Why have You abandoned Me?" Some hours later, Jesus gave another loud cry, took His last breath, and died.

Jesus was the only human being to ever live a perfect life. He did nothing wrong, not ever. He only lived and loved and taught and cared for others. Yet He was beaten and killed for things He did not do. With the power of God, Jesus could have stopped all of this. But on purpose He endured the worst kind of pain and death so that He could save others from their bad actions. This is how much Jesus loves people. This is the greatest story of all time, but the story doesn't end here. . . The story picks back up with an empty tomb!

(Adapted from Matthew 27; Mark 15; Luke 23; John 19)

AN EMPTY TOMB

The Story of Jesus' Resurrection (Part 1)

After Jesus died, all of His followers were very sad. One of them, a rich man named Joseph from Arimathea, asked Pilate if he could bury Jesus' body. Pilate said yes. Joseph was a good man who loved and followed Jesus. He carefully wrapped Jesus' body in linen cloth and put it in a new, empty tomb in a garden near where Jesus had died. Then he rolled a big stone over the doorway of the tomb. Some of Jesus' friends saw all of this happen and wanted to come back later to put spices and perfumes on Jesus' body to honor and care for Him.

Meanwhile, the religious leaders who hated Jesus were worried. They remembered Jesus had promised to rise from the dead after three days. So they said to Pilate, "Put soldiers at Jesus' tomb to guard it, and seal the stone up tight. That way no one can steal Jesus' body away and lie that He rose from the dead."

Very early on the first day of the week, some women who loved and followed Jesus started out on their way back to the tomb. They had their spices and perfumes ready. As they walked they wondered, "Who will roll the big stone away so we can care for Jesus' body?" They knew they certainly were not strong enough.

But when they got to the tomb, they were amazed. The earth shook hard like an earthquake, and an angel came down from heaven! With a mighty push, the angel moved the stone away from Jesus' grave and sat down on the stone. He was as bright as lightning and white as snow. When the guards felt the earth shake and saw the angel, they were terrified and trembling—so terrified and trembling that they dropped to the ground like they were dead.

The women were scared too, but the angel spoke kindly to them. "Don't be afraid," he said. "I know you're looking for Jesus, but He is not here. He rose from the dead just like He promised. Look in the tomb and see that He is gone. Then go tell His followers that He is not dead—He is alive!"

How shocked and excited the women were! Jesus meant it when He said He would rise from the dead. His promise was true. God's promises are *always* true.

(Adapted from Matthew 27–28; Mark 15–16; Luke 23–24; John 19–20)

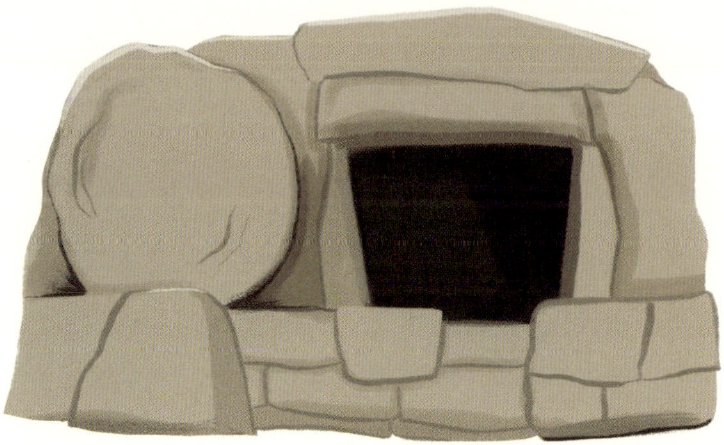

HE LIVES!

The Story of Jesus' Resurrection (Part 2)

The women hurried away from Jesus' empty tomb to do what the angel said. They were afraid but filled with joy and excited to share the incredible news that Jesus was alive. They believed the angel and had seen for themselves that Jesus' dead body was gone from the tomb. Suddenly, Jesus met them on the road so they could see Him face-to-face. "Hello," He said, and oh, how happy the women were! They bowed down to touch His feet and worship Him.

Then Jesus said, "Go and tell My followers to go to Galilee. They will see Me there."

Meanwhile, some of the solider guards who had been at the tomb reported everything they had seen to the religious leaders who hated Jesus. The religious leaders offered the soldiers lots of money to spread lies. They said, "Tell all the people that Jesus' followers came and stole His dead body." The soldiers took the money and spread the lies, and this is why many people even today do not believe that Jesus rose from the dead.

But no matter who believed the lies, the truth was still that Jesus was alive. For the next forty days, Jesus appeared to people and spoke with them, proving He had risen from the dead. He urged His followers to go and share the good news that He would save people from their sin and give eternal life to all who trust in Him.

One night, Jesus' followers were gathered together with all the doors locked, and Jesus miraculously came and stood among them. He showed them the scars where His hands had been nailed to the cross and His side that had been pierced with a spear. And His followers were so happy. One follower, Thomas, was not there that night, and later he said he would never believe until he could see for himself the scars on Jesus' hands and side. Not long after, Jesus came to Thomas and said, "Put your finger into My hands. Put your hand into My side. Stop doubting and believe!" Then Thomas did believe, and Jesus said to him, "Thomas, because you have seen Me, you believe. Blessed are those who have never seen Me and yet believe."

The Bible says that Jesus did many other powerful works in front of His followers. They are not written in the Bible. But the ones that are written in the Bible are there so that you may believe Jesus is the Christ, the Son of God. When you put your trust in Him, you will have life that lasts forever through His name.

This is the greatest story of all time, the truest story of all time, the story that matters the most of all time!

(Adapted from Matthew 28, Mark 16, Luke 24, John 20)

Prayers for Healing

When winter turns to spring, we see beautiful new life. The frozen ground thaws out and welcomes new seeds to get cozy so that they can take root and grow. Plants and flowers and trees that were huddled in tight to survive the cold get nourished by the sunshine and warmer weather, and they begin to emerge and bloom again. The change from winter to spring is wonderful! Many people in Bible times needed help changing too. They had illness and injury and trouble that hurt and held them back. But God has all power to heal and make new, and we see that over and over in the pages of the Bible. Through the accounts of healing recorded in the Bible, we can be inspired to pray for healing for both others and ourselves. Read the following stories and see for yourself!

"TAKE PITY ON US, SON OF DAVID"

Two Men's Prayer for Healing from Blindness

No matter the weather or time of day, no matter if the sun shone bright or if the skies were gray, two men back in Bible times lived in total darkness. They were blind and could not see. And their blindness made their lives hard.

But even though they did not have sight, the two men had hope! They knew of old prophecies that told of a Messiah. This Savior would be from the Jewish family line of David. The book of Isaiah said that He would help those who are blind see and make people happier.

Another prophecy from Isaiah said, "The eyes of people who are blind will be opened. And the ears of those who can't hear will be opened. And those who can't walk will jump like a deer. And those who can't speak will call out for joy."

And yet another one said, "He will open blind eyes. He will bring people out of the prison of darkness."

So when the two men who were blind heard about a man named Jesus who was teaching and preaching and healing people, they wondered, *Could He be the Messiah we've hoped for and dreamed about? Could He fulfill the old prophecies? Could He heal us? Could He make us see?*

Imagine their excitement when they realized Jesus was traveling by their area! "Let's follow Him," they said. And they did. And they cried out to Him, "Take pity on us, Son of David." They even followed Jesus into someone's house. They had to use their senses of hearing and touch to get around carefully, since they couldn't see.

Jesus said to them, "Do you have faith that I can do this?"

"Yes, sir!" they said to Him.

Then Jesus put His hands on their eyes and said, "You will have what you want because of your faith."

And suddenly, their eyes were opened. They could see! Light and colors, people and buildings, trees and birds. . .*everything*! And it was all so beautiful to the two men who once were blind but now could see. The two men were excited! They told everyone they could about Jesus, and news about Him spread all over their country.

God can still heal people. So when you know someone is sick, ask Him to help them get better. He might make them just as happy as the men who were once blind.

(Adapted from Isaiah 29; 35; 42; Matthew 9)

"PLEASE PUT YOUR HAND ON HIM"

A Prayer for a Man Who Couldn't Hear or Speak

He could see, but he could not hear. He could feel, but he could barely talk. What must life have been like for a man who was deaf and couldn't speak back in ancient Bible times? Was he lonely? Did he have a family? Could he work a job? What were his friends like?

The man clearly had people who cared about him because when Jesus traveled back to the Sea of Galilee, those friends brought him to Jesus. They had heard that Jesus could do great miracles—He could heal people who had disabilities and people who were sick and people who were blind. Surely He could heal someone who was deaf and who couldn't speak!

"Please put Your hand on him," the man's friends begged Jesus.

Jesus must have wanted some space. He took the man a bit away from the other people. He put his fingers into the man's ears. Then Jesus spit on His own finger and put it on the man's tongue. Next, Jesus looked up to heaven and breathed deeply from within. "Be opened!" He said.

At once the man's ears were opened! He was no longer deaf! He could hear everything! At once the man's tongue was made loose! He could now speak just like other people! What sounds did he notice first? Did he hear the gasps and happy cries of his friends who had just witnessed the miracle of his healing? What words did he use right away? Did he say a great big "Thank You!" to Jesus?

Jesus told the people there that they shouldn't tell anyone about the miracle. But the more He told people this, the more they talked about what He had done. They were very

surprised and wondered why they should keep Jesus' miracles a secret. They said, "He has done all things well. He helps people hear. He helps people speak."

"Please put Your hand on him," the man's friends had begged of Jesus. We can beg Jesus to put His hand on us and our loved ones today too. We can trust that He always does all things well.

(Adapted from Mark 7)

"LORD, YOU CAN HEAL ME!"

A Man's Prayer for Healing from Leprosy

Itchy, scabby spots and sores—*ewww*—no one wants those! But many people in Bible times suffered from skin diseases and needed healing. And there were not hospitals and clinics and doctors all around. Leprosy was a well-known skin disease—and it was terrible. People who had it were avoided by others who feared catching it. Sometimes these people were banished from their homes and towns and cities and sent to live in caves along with other people who had leprosy. It was rare that anyone wanted to help them. No one knew how to cure and heal leprosy.

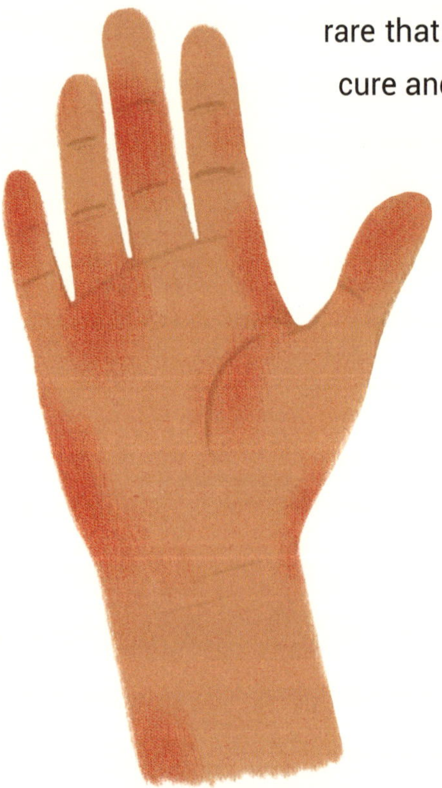

No one but Jesus. He knew how to cure and heal, and He was not afraid of skin diseases.

One day Jesus came down from a mountainside, and large crowds of people followed Him. Soon a man with leprosy came to Jesus and got down on his knees before Jesus to worship Him. The man said, "Lord, if You will, You can heal me!"

And Jesus put His hand on him and said, "I will. You are healed!"

At once the man was healed. No more scabs or spots or sores!

Jesus could have simply said the words, "You're

healed." He didn't have to place His hand on the man with leprosy. But He did. Jesus showed great compassion and care to a man no one else would touch or even go near.

Jesus said to the man, "Go now, but tell no one. Let the religious leader see you. This will show them you have been healed." The law in those days said people who had been healed of leprosy had to be examined by a religious leader to be declared clean. Only then could they return to their home and neighbors. How clean and fresh and new the man healed of leprosy must have felt! How happy he must have been to get to see people up close again.

Jesus comes to those who need healing and help. He gives them great love and care and is willing to touch and restore those who have faith in Him. In any illness or injury, always remember that Jesus alone is worthy of the prayer, "Lord, You can heal me!"

(Adapted from Matthew 8)

"O GOD, HEAL HER, I PRAY!"

Moses' Prayer for Miriam

Brothers and sisters don't always get along well. They fight and argue sometimes. That was just as common in Bible times as it is today. One day Moses and his brother, Aaron, and their sister, Miriam, were in the middle of an argument. They weren't kids anymore either. They were all grown up! Aaron and Miriam spoke against Moses because they disagreed about the woman he'd chosen to marry. And then they were full of pride, saying, "Is it true that the Lord has spoken *only* through Moses? Has He not spoken through us also?"

God hears everything, and He heard them. And God knows everything too. They couldn't hide their pride from God. But Moses was a man with no pride. He was not full of a bragging, better-than-everyone-else attitude. He thought of others more than himself. He was the humblest man on earth. And when God heard the prideful things that Aaron and Miriam were saying, He said to Moses and Aaron and Miriam, "You three come out to the meeting tent."

So the three of them went out. Then the Lord came down in a cloud and stood at the door of the meeting tent. He called to Aaron and Miriam. When both of them came near, God said, "Now listen to Me. My servant Moses is faithful in all My house. He is the only one I speak with face-to-face. And he is the only one who sees what the Lord is like. So why weren't you afraid to speak against My servant Moses?"

God was angry with them, and He left. And when the cloud lifted from over the meeting tent, Miriam had leprosy—that very bad skin disease. It turned her skin as white as snow! Everyone would be afraid to catch it from her. Would they run away from her? Would she die from the leprosy?

Even though the siblings had quarreled, they loved one another, and Aaron was scared for his sister. He saw her skin disease and said to Moses, "Oh, I beg you. We don't want to be punished because we have been foolish and have sinned. Don't let Miriam suffer with this skin disease!"

Moses knew the matter was in God's hands. He cried out to the Lord, saying, "O God, heal her, I pray!"

And God listened to Moses. He had mercy on Miriam because of her brother's prayer.

(Adapted from Numbers 12)

APRIL

Spring Blooms

If you've ever planted a garden, you know that a good and healthy garden changes and grows. Tiny seeds lie down in soft soil beds and get all covered up and cozy. And then a miracle begins—a miracle only the one true Creator God can do. The seeds break open and new life begins, pushing up through the soil toward the sunshine, blooming and producing good things—flowers, strawberries, potatoes, carrots, beans. . .

If a seed only ever stayed in its bed of soil, how sad! No one would ever see what it was capable of producing, what beautiful flower or tree or tasty fruit or vegetable it would become.

Like seeds, to be good and healthy and produce what we are meant to, every person needs to grow and bloom—most importantly in faith and friendship with our Creator God and Savior Jesus Christ.

The Bible is full of examples of real-life people who grew and bloomed in their faith, and even though they lived a long time ago, their stories can inspire us right now to be like them—no matter our age or season of life. Read the following stories and see for yourself!

AN EPIC TRUST IN GOD

The Story of Gideon

During the time of judges in the Bible, God's people of Israel spent seven years under the power of the nation of Midian. God let this happen because Israel had turned away from God. Midian was much stronger than Israel, and Midian was very cruel to Israel. The Midianites stole and destroyed food and animals from the Israelites every chance they could. So Israel became very poor and very weak, and they cried out to God for help.

God sent a prophet to remind the people of Israel that even though God had done so much for them in the past, still they had disobeyed Him and worshipped other gods.

The angel of the Lord appeared to an Israelite man named Gideon as he was working to keep food hidden from the Midianites.

The angel said to Gideon, "The Lord is with you, mighty hero!"

Gideon replied, "Then why has all this happened to us? The Lord has left us alone and put us under the power of the Midianites."

And the Lord said, "You are strong and you can rescue Israel from the Midianites. I am sending you."

Gideon couldn't believe his ears. "How can I rescue Israel?" he said. "I'm nobody special. My family is the least powerful in our tribe, and I am the least in my family."

But the Lord said, "I will be with you, and you will destroy Midian."

Gideon still wasn't so sure about all this, and he asked the Lord to prove it was truly Him speaking. Gideon brought bread and meat and put it on a rock, and the angel of the Lord touched it with the tip of his staff. Then fire burned up all the bread and meat and the angel disappeared, and Gideon knew the angel was truly from God.

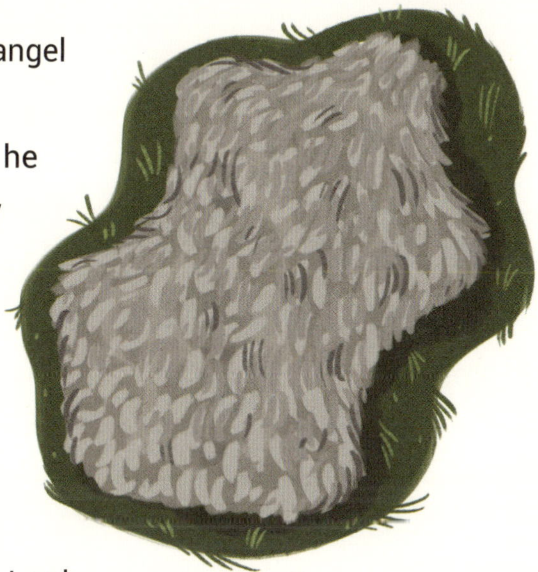

Two more times as Gideon obeyed God, he asked God to show him proof that it was truly Him. Gideon laid out a wool fleece and asked God to make it wet with dew the next morning but all the rest of the ground dry. And God did. Then Gideon laid out a wool fleece again and asked God to keep it dry the next morning while all the ground around it was wet. And God did.

Gideon was filled with powerful faith, and the Lord kept speaking to him to show him how to defeat the Midianites.

Gideon started with an army of thirty-two thousand men, but twenty-two thousand left. They were too scared to fight. Then God told Gideon He wanted only three hundred men to fight against the powerful Midianites, to prove that all the real power came from God alone. So, with God's power, Gideon and the army of only three hundred men rescued Israel from under the power of Midian.

Gideon was just an ordinary man doing ordinary things—in the beginning. But by trusting God and growing in faith, Gideon went on to do *extraordinary* things.

(Adapted from Judges 6–7)

FOR SUCH A TIME AS THIS

The Story of Esther

One day long ago in the country of Persia, a king named Xerxes decided to host a huge banquet party. King Xerxes loved to show off how rich and extravagant he was. He ordered his wife, Queen Vashti, to come to his party for everyone to see. But she didn't want to, so she didn't—and that made King Xerxes very, very mad. He was so mad that he issued a royal decree that Queen Vashti could not be near him ever again and that another queen would take her place.

When King Xerxes began searching for a new queen, his servants gathered many beautiful women from all areas of their country. Among them all, a woman named Esther was the most beautiful and kind, and King Xerxes liked her best. So he chose Esther to be queen instead of Vashti.

Esther was a Jewish woman, but she had kept her family history a secret. Her parents had died, and she was raised by her cousin named Mordecai, who took good care of her and kept watch over her. He didn't want her to be mistreated for being Jewish.

Meanwhile, a man named Haman was given a high position among King Xerxes' leaders. Haman was not a good man, and he wanted all people to bow down and honor him. Mordecai refused to bow down to anyone but God. Because of this, Haman was filled with hate for Jewish people, and he convinced King Xerxes to order a decree to have them all killed.

Mordecai got word to Esther about what was going on. He urged her to go to the king and beg for mercy for the Jewish people.

But Esther said, "If I go to the king without being invited, I will be killed. The only exception is if the king extends his scepter and spares my life."

And Mordecai said, "If you are silent, help will come to the Jews from another way, but you and your father's family will die. So who knows, but maybe you became queen to help at exactly a time like this!"

So Esther asked Mordecai to gather all the Jews to fast and pray for her. Then after three days, Esther went to the king. He did not turn her away but held out his scepter and welcomed her. Her life was spared, and soon she was able to show the king how evil Haman was. Eventually Haman was killed, and King Xerxes stopped the decree to kill all Jewish people. Even better, he decreed that Jewish people could protect themselves and fight against any of their enemies.

Because of Esther's growth in faith and courage, she allowed God to work through her to save her entire nation of people.

(Adapted from the book of Esther)

A GREAT SACRIFICE

The Story of Abraham and Isaac

Abraham was a man called a friend of God. He and his wife, Sarah, were shocked when God promised they would have a baby boy. They thought they were much too old to have children. But God's promises are always true, and their son, Isaac, was born when Abraham was one hundred years old and Sarah was ninety years old. Isaac's name meant "laughter" because Sarah had laughed in disbelief when God said she would have a son in her old age. But God had responded, "Is anything too hard for the Lord?"

Some years later, God had a test for Abraham. He asked Abraham to prove his love and obedience to God by offering his son Isaac as a sacrifice.

As hard as it was, Abraham chose to obey. He trusted God's promises. He took two servants and Isaac, and they went together to cut up wood for the fire for their offering. Then they set out toward the mountain where God instructed Abraham to go give the sacrifice. On the third day of traveling, Abraham told his servants to stay back while he and Isaac traveled ahead together. As they went on, Isaac said to his dad, "We have the wood and fire, but where is the lamb for the offering?"

Abraham answered, "God Himself will provide the lamb."

When they reached the right place, Abraham built an altar and placed the wood on top. Then he tied up Isaac and laid him on the altar. At the very last moment, the angel of the Lord stopped Abraham, saying, "Don't hurt him. Now I see that you truly respect God, because you were willing to give up your only son."

Then Abraham looked in the bushes and saw a ram caught by its horns there. Here

was the sacrifice to give instead of Isaac! And so Abraham named the place "The Lord Will Provide."

Then the angel of the Lord said to Abraham, "You have not kept your only son from me. Because of this I will bless you and your descendants and make them as many as the stars in the sky and the sand on the shores! Through your children all nations on earth will be blessed because you have obeyed me."

Abraham grew during this difficult test. His trust and faith deepened because he loved God and had seen God show Himself as the perfect provider. Abraham truly was a "friend of God."

(Adapted from Genesis 17:1–18:15; 22:1–18; Hebrews 11:17–19)

ONE THING THAT'S NEEDED

The Story of Mary and Martha

On one of Jesus' many journeys, He stopped in a tiny village called Bethany on a slope of the Mount of Olives. A woman named Martha welcomed Jesus into her home. She was excited and had many things to do to get ready for their special guest. She wanted to make Jesus feel comfortable and offer Him a nice place to rest and relax. A delicious meal was a must as well!

Martha was very good at hosting guests, and she knew all the details of planning and preparing for a visitor. She knew those details too well actually—because they soon began to distract her from the importance and blessing of such a wonderful guest.

Martha's sister named Mary was also at Martha's house at the time of Jesus' visit. Mary did not join Martha in the work of hosting. She chose to simply sit at Jesus' feet and listen to everything He had to say. This made Martha mad. It upset her so much that she said to Jesus, "Lord, do You see that I am doing all the work here by myself? Do You see that my sister is just sitting around? Do You care? Tell her to help me!"

Jesus loved both sisters, and He wanted Martha to learn and grow from Mary's example. He replied, "Martha, Martha, you are upset about so many things, but there is just one thing that's needed. Mary has chosen that one thing. She has chosen what is better, and it will not be taken from her."

What is that one thing? Martha wondered. *What did my sister choose that is better?* And then Martha understood. Simply being with Jesus and listening was far better than frantically working to serve Him. Martha's fussing had taken her focus away from where it needed to be—fixed on Jesus. But no more. She would remember Mary's example. She would remember that she should serve Jesus with love and wisdom without being caught up in the details. She would remember to relax and enjoy just spending time with Jesus. And she knew that in remembering these things, she would grow in her faith and relationship with the Savior.

(Adapted from Luke 10:38–42)

Prayers to Bring the Dead Back to Life

Death isn't fun to think about. Anyone who has ever lost a family member or friend knows how sad it is. It's hard to lose someone you love so much and have to learn to live without them. But even though death is sad and scary, God has the superpower over it! And Eastertime is when we celebrate that. God alone can bring people back from death to life. And because His Son, Jesus, took our sin when He died on the cross and was raised to life again, you can trust that you will also rise to life again after death if you admit your sin and believe in Jesus as your Savior. Have you done that so you will live forever? Pray to God and let Him give you that gift. Have all your family and friends done that so they will live forever? Pray for them to trust Jesus as Savior and receive new life too. Meanwhile, keep loving God well as you live here on earth. Ask Him to show you the good things He created you for. Keep learning about God through His Word, and let the Bible remind you that God alone has the power to bring the dead back to life. Read the following stories and see for yourself!

"FATHER, I THANK YOU FOR HEARING ME"

Jesus' Prayer for the Resurrection of Lazarus

When Jesus lived on earth, three of His dearest friends were Mary, Martha, and Lazarus. They were siblings who lived together in a town called Bethany. When Lazarus became very ill, Mary and Martha were scared for their brother. They knew he might die. So they sent word to Jesus, who was traveling. When Jesus heard his friend Lazarus was sick, He stayed two more days where He was but then said to His disciples, "Let's go into the country of Judea again." That's where Bethany was.

The disciples were afraid for Jesus because people in Judea had tried to kill Him. They said, "Teacher, the Jews tried to throw stones at You to kill You there not long ago. Are You really going to Judea again?"

Jesus said that He was. As He traveled, He learned that Lazarus had died and been buried.

The grave where Lazarus was buried was a hole in the side of a hill. A stone covered the door. When Jesus got there, He said, "Take the stone away." But Martha said to Him, "Lord, by now his body has a bad smell. He has been dead four days."

And Jesus said to her, "Did I not say that if you would believe, you would see the greatness of God?"

So they took the stone away. Jesus looked up and said, "Father, I thank You for hearing Me. I know You always hear Me. But I said that so the people standing here would believe You have sent Me." Then He called with a loud voice, "Lazarus, come out!"

And Lazarus did! His hands and feet and face and body were all tied up and covered in graveclothes, so Jesus said to the people, "Take off the graveclothes and let him go." The man who had been dead for four days was alive and well again!

Jesus had told Martha, "Your brother will rise again. I am the one who raises the dead and gives them life. Anyone who trusts in Me will live again and never die. Do you believe this?" Martha answered, "Yes, Lord, I believe that You are the Christ, the Son of God, who has come into the world."

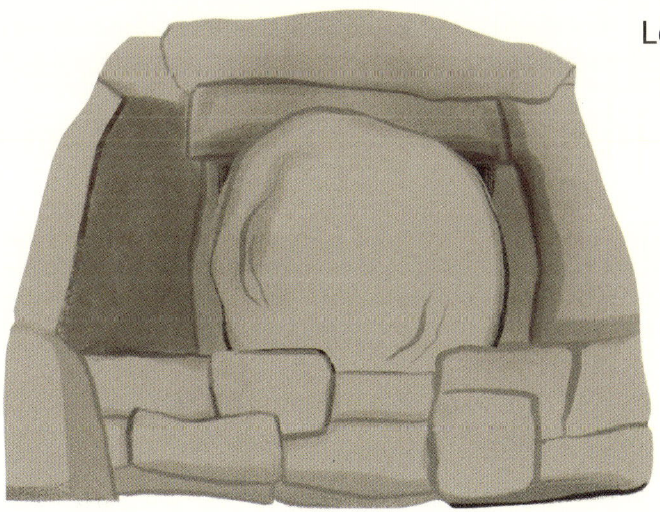

Jesus proved Himself true when He raised Lazarus from the dead. And we prove ourselves faithful to Jesus today by continuing to believe in Jesus like Martha did.

(Adapted from John 11)

"GET UP, TABITHA!"

Peter's Prayer for Tabitha's Resurrection

A woman named Tabitha was a follower of Jesus. She lived in the town of Joppa and was known for being good and kind and making lovely clothing for others to wear—beautiful tunics and other things that were stylish back then. When she became sick and then died, her friends were very sad. They had loved her so much and had appreciated how giving she was to others.

Tabitha's friends washed and prepared her body, in the customs of their day, and laid her in a room on the second floor of a house. But even though she had died, her friends still had hope. They knew of a special man who also loved and followed Jesus—a man named Peter. He had been Jesus' disciple not that long ago when Jesus lived on earth. This was the same Peter who had asked Jesus to help him walk on water! And now Peter was known to heal the sick and raise the dead back to life in Jesus' name.

Tabitha's friends had heard Peter was traveling through a town nearby. So two of Tabitha's friends went to Peter and begged him to come and help Tabitha. "Hurry, please!" they urged him. "Our dear friend has died, but we have heard of you, and we believe you can help."

Peter agreed to come with them, and he went to the house where they had laid Tabitha's body. Her friends were gathered around her, weeping and crying, for they missed their dear friend. They showed Peter all the nice clothing she had made them.

Then Peter told them to leave the room, and he knelt and prayed to God. Peter was full of faith. He had seen with his own eyes the many miracles of Jesus, and he prayed

to God knowing that all miracles come from Him.

Then he said to Tabitha, "Get up, Tabitha!" And she opened her eyes and looked at Peter and sat up! He took her by the hand and helped her get up. Then he presented her to all her friends and the people gathered there to show them God had raised Tabitha from death to life. Imagine how happy they were! Imagine how they must have hugged and kissed her. Imagine how their tears of sadness turned to tears of joy. After all the excitement, Tabitha probably went right back to doing the many good and kind things she loved to do.

News of Tabitha being brought back to life spread throughout Joppa. And because of that incredible news, many people put their trust in Jesus. Have you put your trust in Him? If not, He would love to be part of your life!

(Adapted from Acts 9:36–42)

"LET THIS CHILD'S LIFE RETURN TO HIM"

Elijah's Prayer for the Resurrection of the Widow's Son

The prophet Elijah spoke messages from God. One day he warned King Ahab, "There will be no rain for the next few years." Without water, plants and food would not grow, and animals and people would die.

Ahab was a very bad king who did not honor God, and he did not like this warning. So God told Elijah, "Leave here and hide from King Ahab by the river. Drink from the river. I have told the ravens to bring you food to eat."

Elijah obeyed. He had food and water just as God promised. But after a while, the river dried up because there was no rain in the land.

Then God told Elijah, "Go to the town called Zarephath. I have told a woman there to feed you." Again, Elijah obeyed. When he came to the city, he saw a woman gathering sticks. He said, "Could you get me a little water in a jar so I can have a drink?" She agreed, and then Elijah asked, "Could you also bring me a piece of bread to eat?"

But to that she said, "I have no bread—only a little flour and oil. See, I am gathering sticks to bake something small for me and my son, and after we eat it we will starve."

Elijah said, "Don't be afraid. Go and do as you have said. But make me a little loaf of bread first. For God says, 'The jar of flour will not be used up. The jar of oil will not be empty, until the day the Lord sends rain down on the earth.'"

So the woman did what Elijah said. And she and her son and Elijah ate for many days! The jar of flour was not used up, and the jar of oil did not become empty. It happened just like God had said.

Before long, though, the woman's son grew sick and died. She cried and was angry. But Elijah said, "Give me your son." He carried the boy to a bedroom, laid him down on a bed, and prayed, "O Lord, let this child's life return to him." God listened. The child came back to life and became strong again! Imagine how his mother must have celebrated!

She knew that God was real and His Word was true. From her story, and from the work of God in our own lives, we can believe that too.

(Adapted from 1 Kings 17)

"LORD, REMEMBER HOW I HAVE WALKED WITH YOU"

Hezekiah's Prayer for a Longer Life

Hezekiah was a king of Judah who did what was good and right and true. He wanted to obey God with his whole heart. Because of that, all went well for Hezekiah.

But even good people can still get sick. One day Hezekiah got very sick. The prophet Isaiah came to him and said, "This is what the Lord says: 'Get those of your house ready. For you will die. You will not get well again.'"

But Hezekiah had hope. He knew he could still ask God to give him a longer life. He turned his face to the wall and prayed, "Lord, remember how I have walked with You in truth and with my whole heart. I have done what is good in Your eyes." Then Hezekiah began to cry.

God was listening to Hezekiah. The Lord heard his cries and saw his tears. So before Isaiah had even left the room, God told him, "Tell Hezekiah, 'This is what the Lord says: "I have heard your prayer. I have seen your tears. And I will heal you. On the third day you must go up to the house of the Lord. And I will add fifteen years to your life."'"

Then Isaiah said to the king's servants, "Get some figs and make them into a loaf. Lay that loaf on the sore on Hezekiah's body. Then he will be well again." They did, and Hezekiah was healed! God answered Hezekiah's prayer for a longer life.

Hezekiah then asked Isaiah how he would know that he was truly healed when he went to the temple as God had instructed. He asked, "What will be the special thing for me to see?"

Isaiah answered, "The special thing for you to see is up to you. Would you like the sun's shadow to go ten steps farther or to go back ten steps?"

Hezekiah replied, "It's easy for the shadow to go ten steps farther. Let the shadow turn back ten steps." So Isaiah asked God to change the shadows as a sign for Hezekiah, and God did!

God heard and answered Hezekiah's prayer for new life. God heard and answered Isaiah's prayer for a sign for Hezekiah. God hears and answers our prayers today too, especially when we walk with Him in truth and serve Him with our whole hearts.

(Adapted from 2 Kings 20)

MAY

Celebration of Mothers

Only a mother can have two beating hearts at once. Isn't that incredible? (Or maybe more than two if she is carrying twins or triplets. . .or more. Wow!) Only a mother can be her own unique person and yet carry a totally unique and new person inside her tummy too. Amazing! God sure made mothers extraspecial people. From the very first second of life, a mother cares for her children, cradled safely inside her belly, growing and changing until the day they are ready to be born. And then a good mother continues to care for her children's needs as babies and toddlers and so on until they are all grown up. Truly she never stops caring for them no matter how old they are. What a blessing good mothers are. At every time of year, hug yours—or someone who is like a mother to you—tight, and tell her thank you for everything she does for you every chance you get. And especially during the month of May, when we have the holiday of Mother's Day, we should appreciate, honor, and celebrate the good moms in our lives.

The Bible blesses us with wonderful examples of good mothers who loved their children well. We can learn from their lives and appreciate, honor, and celebrate them too. Read the following stories and see for yourself!

A PERSISTENT PRAYER

The Story of Hannah

A woman named Hannah in the Bible desperately wanted to be a mother, but she had no children. It broke her heart to not have any babies. Every year she traveled with her husband to a place called Shiloh during a special time of feasting and celebrating to worship God and bring Him gifts. And every year Hannah cried and prayed, asking God to bless her with a son. Sometimes she felt like God had forgotten her or didn't care about how sad she was. But still Hannah kept praying. She promised God, "Oh mighty Lord, if You will give me a son, I will give him back to You for all the days of his life."

A religious leader named Eli was sitting near the temple of the Lord. He watched Hannah praying and wondered what was wrong.

Hannah told him, "I am very sad and am crying out to God."

Eli told her, "Go peacefully, and may the God of Israel give you what you have asked."

Right away, Hannah felt much better. Her heart no longer felt so broken. She went home with her husband, and soon she did have a baby boy! She named him Samuel, saying, "I asked the Lord for him."

Hannah dearly loved and cared for baby Samuel, but she never forgot her prayers and her promise to God. When the little boy was old enough to eat on his own, Hannah returned to Shiloh to the temple where she had met Eli. There she told Eli, "I asked for my son, and God gave him to me. So now I give him back to God for his whole life." Hannah meant she was letting Samuel live at the temple to grow up and be a servant of God there under the care of Eli.

Every year, Hannah came back to the temple to visit Samuel. And God blessed Hannah with three more sons and two daughters. She was greatly rewarded for being faithful to the Lord.

One night, when Samuel was still very young, he woke up to someone calling his name. He thought it was Eli and went to him, saying, "Here I am."

Eli said, "I didn't call for you. Go back to sleep."

But then it happened again. And again.

Finally Eli said, "It's not me calling you. It must be the Lord." He instructed Samuel to go back and lie down and to say, "Speak to me. Your servant is listening," if he heard God's voice again.

And the Lord did call Samuel again, and Samuel listened. Samuel continued to listen and grew to be a very important leader and speaker for God. He was a blessing to all the people of Israel because Hannah was a wonderful mother who trusted God and kept her promise to Him about her son.

(Adapted from 1 Samuel 1–3)

BABY IN A BASKET

The Story of Jochebed

When God's people, the Israelites, lived in Egypt, a king called Pharaoh decided there were too many of them. He was afraid the Israelites would join together to take away his power. So he made all the Israelites slaves, and he made sure they were treated cruelly. Pharaoh even ordered that every new baby boy born to an Israelite mother must be killed. But the midwives, the women who helped new moms as they delivered their babies, feared God and secretly refused to kill babies. They made up stories to tell Pharaoh to keep protecting the baby boys, and God blessed them for their love and courage.

But then Pharaoh said, "Every Israelite baby boy who is born must be thrown into the Nile River!"

Jochebed was one of the Israelite women who gave birth to a baby boy during Pharaoh's cruel reign. She loved and cared for her son and kept him safe for three months. But as he grew, he became too big to hide. She was afraid he'd be thrown into the Nile River to die. So she came up with a plan. Jochebed covered a basket with tar and pitch, materials that would make the basket float upon the water. Then she gently put her baby boy inside the basket and put it among the reeds near the edge of the Nile River. She knew that Pharaoh's daughter often came to bathe in the water there. Jochebed asked her daughter, Miriam, to watch over the baby in the basket and see what happened.

Soon, the princess spotted the basket and looked inside. She found the poor little baby crying and felt sorry for him. She realized the tiny boy was one of the babies her father had ordered to die.

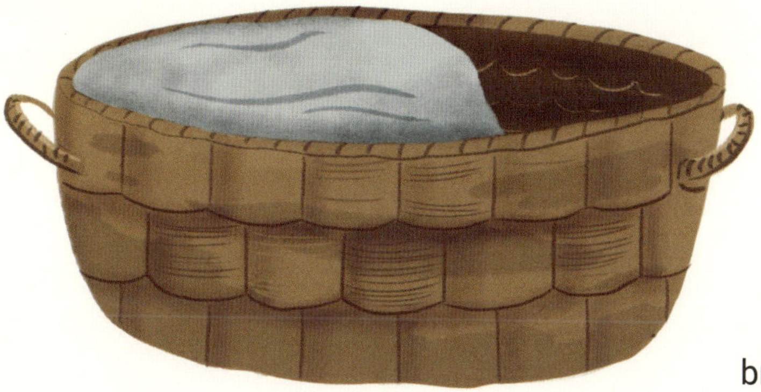

Then Miriam came to the princess and asked, "Do you want me to find a mother who can feed him for you?"

And the princess agreed. So Miriam brought Jochebed to the princess.

The princess said, "I will pay you to take care of him for me until he can eat on his own." She had no idea she was talking to the baby's real mother! But God knew.

Jochebed happily agreed. She had hidden and protected her son from being killed, and she was now able to keep him and care for him awhile longer.

When the baby grew old enough, Jochebed gave him back to Pharaoh's daughter. The princess named him Moses, saying, "I took him out of the water."

Jochebed's heart must have hurt to give up her son, but more important than her own heart was protecting her child. Because of his mother's courage, Moses' life was saved from Pharaoh's evil plans, and Moses grew to be one of the greatest leaders of all time.

(Adapted from Exodus 2:1–10)

UNLIKELY MOTHER

The Story of Elizabeth

Elizabeth was the wife of a priest, a Jewish religious leader named Zechariah. They lived in the time of King Herod in Judea. Both Zechariah and Elizabeth loved God with all their hearts and did their best to obey Him in all things. But they had not been blessed with children, and they were both growing older.

One day, Zechariah went into the temple of the Lord to burn incense to honor God. Suddenly an angel of the Lord appeared to him. Zechariah was surprised and afraid.

But the angel said, "Do not be afraid, Zechariah. God has heard your prayer, and your wife is going to have your son. Name him John. He will fill you with joy, and not just you but many people will have joy because of him. For he will be great in God's eyes. He is never to drink wine, and he will be filled with the Holy Spirit the moment he is born. Because of him, many people of Israel will come back to following the Lord their God. He will help people obey God and be ready for Him."

What a special son, indeed! Zechariah could hardly believe it. He asked, "How is this possible? My wife and I are too old to have children."

The angel said, "I am Gabriel. I stand in the presence of God and have been sent to tell you this good news. Now you will be unable to speak until your son is born because you did not believe my words, which will come true at just the right time."

Zechariah came out of the temple, and the people wondered why he couldn't speak. He kept making signs with his hands, and the people realized he must have had a vision in the temple.

Soon, his wife Elizabeth did become pregnant, just as Gabriel had promised. She was amazed and happy and said, "The Lord has done this for me."

When Elizabeth was six months pregnant, the same angel Gabriel went to tell another mother, Mary, that she would also have a very special baby boy. The most special of all, actually—Jesus! Elizabeth and Mary were cousins, and so baby John and baby Jesus were cousins too. Mary went to visit Elizabeth soon after Gabriel visited her, and the moment Elizabeth heard Mary's voice, baby John inside her belly leaped with joy! Elizabeth was filled with the Holy Spirit and said to Mary, "You are blessed among women, and blessed is the child you are carrying. Blessed are the women who believe that what the Lord has said will happen!"

Beautiful, faithful mothers like Elizabeth and Mary believe God for what seems impossible, and in so doing they are greatly blessed.

(Adapted from Luke 1)

A LOVING MOTHER-IN-LAW

The Story of Naomi

Mothers gain new children when their own children grow up and get married. Naomi was a mother-in-law who had a daughter-in-law named Ruth. And Ruth was all she had left because her husband and two sons had died, and one daughter-in-law had gone back to her own family. But Ruth so loved Naomi that she was determined to stay with her, even when it would have been safer for Ruth to go home to her people to try to find a new husband. Ruth said to her mother-in-law, "I want to go where you go. I want to stay where you stay. I want your people to be my people. I want your God to be my God. I never want to leave you as long as I am alive."

And so Naomi shared her life with her daughter-in-law. And most importantly, she shared her faith in God. After they'd traveled together from Moab to Bethlehem, God led Ruth to the fields owned by a kind and good man named Boaz. When Boaz heard about Ruth's loyalty and love for her mother-in-law, he greatly admired her. He protected and provided for Ruth and Naomi by allowing Ruth to safely gather food in his fields. Ruth came home from her work each day and shared with her mother-in-law about the events of the day. As time went on, Naomi gave Ruth good advice to go to Boaz according to Israelite custom and law to show him she wanted him to be her kinsman-redeemer—her relative to care for her.

Boaz had great integrity; he wanted to do everything in the correct and honorable way according to his people's customs and laws. So once he made sure all was well in taking Ruth as his wife, he married her to care for her and share life with her completely.

Naomi's and Ruth's faith in God, their desire to do right, and their deep bond with each other blessed them beyond what they had imagined. Before long, Ruth and Boaz had a baby boy, a son named Obed. And Naomi was suddenly not just a beloved mother-in-law but a beloved grandmother too.

(Adapted from the book of Ruth)

Prayers of Mothers

In May, the month of Mother's Day, we honor and celebrate our moms and those who are like mothers to us. We give them presents and make them treats; we hug them tight and kiss their cheeks! We let them know what a blessing they are to us and tell them all the things we appreciate about them. We should especially appreciate a mom who prays! A loving mom who prays for her children is an extraspecial treasure. Her prayers are so heartfelt and important. She wants the very best for her children, and she prays to God to ask for His blessings and protection and good gifts for them. She loves to take care of her children, but she knows that sometimes she can't. She also knows that it's really *God* who takes care of them in all things. We can learn from what God's Word shares with us about Bible-time mothers and their prayers for their children. Read the following stories and see for yourself!

"DON'T FORGET ME!"

Hannah's Prayer for a Son

A woman named Hannah, who lived in ancient Bible times, really wanted to be a mother. But she and her husband had no children together. She cried and prayed, asking God to let her have a baby boy. She felt so heartbroken and jealous when she saw other women having children. Sometimes she felt like God had forgotten her or didn't care about her. Her husband would say to her, "Hannah, why are you crying and not eating? And why is your heart sad? Am I not better to you than ten sons?"

But still Hannah kept praying. "Don't forget me, God!" she said. "Look at how troubled and sad I am, and please give me a son." She even made Him a big, important promise, saying, "If You give me a son, I will give him back to You for all the days of his life." She meant that if God gave her a son, then she would let her son live at the temple to grow up and be a servant of God.

One day, a religious leader named Eli was sitting at the door of the temple, and he watched Hannah. He could see Hannah's lips moving, but she made no sounds. At first, he didn't understand what she was doing or what was wrong with her. He thought she might have been drinking. "Put away the wine!" he told her.

"No, I'm not drunk!" Hannah told Eli. "I am troubled in my spirit. I was speaking to the Lord quietly in my heart."

Then Eli said, "Go in peace, and may the God of Israel give you what you asked Him for."

Right away, Hannah felt much better. Her face was no longer sad. She went home with her husband, and soon she did have a baby boy! She named him Samuel, saying,

"I asked the Lord for him."

Sometimes, like Hannah, we might feel as though God has forgotten us. But that is never true. He knows us and remembers us. He loves us and listens to our prayers.

(Adapted from 1 Samuel 1)

"MY HEART IS HAPPY IN THE LORD!"

Hannah's Prayer of Gratitude

Hannah loved baby Samuel so much, and she took good care of him. But she never forgot her prayers and her promise to God. When the little boy was old enough, Hannah went back to the temple where she had met Eli. She said to Eli, "I am the woman you saw praying to the Lord. I asked for my son, and God gave him to me. So now I give him back to God for his whole life." She was letting Samuel live at the temple, where Eli would take care of him. There, Samuel would grow up and be a servant of God.

It was not easy for Hannah to leave Samuel at the temple. She would miss him living at home. Still, Hannah was grateful to God for answering her prayer and blessing her with a son. So she prayed, "My heart is happy in the Lord! My mouth speaks against those who hate me. I have joy in the Lord's saving power. There is no one holy like the Lord. For sure, there is no one better."

She went on to pray more powerful words, saying, "The Lord is a God who knows. He weighs our actions. He kills and brings to life. He raises people from the dead. The Lord makes people poor and rich. But He lifts the poor from the dust. And He lifts those in need from the ashes. He gives them a seat of honor next to rulers. He created the world, and He watches over it and His good people. Those who fight against the Lord will not win. He will give power to His chosen one."

Every year, Hannah came back to the temple to visit Samuel. And God blessed Hannah with three more sons and two daughters. She was rewarded for being faithful to the Lord.

Samuel grew up to become a very important leader and speaker for God. He was a blessing to all the people of Israel because Hannah kept her promise to God about her son.

We can ask God for all kinds of things, but He is most likely to give us the things that help other people. Don't ever be afraid to ask God for good things. Then be sure to use them to make the world a better place.

(Adapted from 1 Samuel 1–2)

"TAKE PITY ON ME, LORD"

A Mother's Prayer for Her Daughter

In Bible times, Tyre and Sidon were cities known for their wickedness. Yet some people from these places wanted to hear from Jesus. They would come in crowds to hear Him preach and teach.

One day, a woman came to ask for Jesus' help. She cried out to Him, "Take pity on me, Lord, Son of David! My daughter has a demon and is very troubled."

To have a demon in Bible times was terrible. The demon somehow controlled the girl's mind and body. Still, this mother loved her daughter dearly. And she believed that Jesus could rescue the girl from the demon.

At first, Jesus did not speak a word to the mother. His friends, the disciples, wondered why. If Jesus wasn't going to help her, they wanted her to leave them alone. So they urged Jesus, "Send her away! She keeps calling us."

Jesus replied, "I was only sent to help the Jewish people who are lost."

Then the mother got down before Jesus. She said, "Lord, help me!" Though she was not Jewish, she believed Jesus was worthy of worship. She believed Jesus alone could help her daughter.

Then Jesus said something strange: "It is not right to take the children's bread and throw it to the dogs." He was not being mean. Jesus was testing the woman to see what her response would be. He wanted to know that her faith in Him was real.

She passed that test with her reply: "Yes, Lord, but even dogs eat the pieces that fall from their owners' tables."

At that clever and faith-filled response, Jesus said to her, "You have much faith. So you will have what you asked for." And her daughter was healed at that very moment. Jesus didn't even have to go see or touch the woman's daughter. He simply spoke the words, and the demon was gone!

Jesus was doing more than testing the mother's faith. He was also teaching everyone who was watching. In that time, Jews often called anyone who was not Jewish a dog. So Jesus was showing that while He came *first* to God's chosen ones, the Jewish people of Israel, He also came for *all* people who choose to believe in Him. It didn't matter then what land or people they were from—and it doesn't matter now. Jesus came to save us all.

(Adapted from Matthew 15; Mark 7)

"SAY THAT MY TWO SONS MAY SIT WITH YOU"

Salome's Prayer for Her Sons

Do you remember that two of Jesus' disciples, the brothers James and John, were called the Sons of Thunder by Jesus? They had been fishermen, just like their father, Zebedee, but they left their boats and nets to become disciples of Jesus when He called them.

The mother of the Sons of Thunder was bold too. Her name was Salome. One day Salome came to Jesus with her sons and got down on her knees before Him to ask something.

So Jesus said to her, "What do you want?"

She replied, "Say that my two sons may sit with You, one at Your right side and one at Your left side, when You are King."

Jesus said to her, "You do not know what you are asking." And to James and John, He asked, "Are you able to take the suffering that I am about to take?"

The Sons of Thunder said, "Yes, we are able."

Jesus said to them, "You will suffer as I will suffer. But the places at My side are not Mine to give. Whoever My Father says will have those places."

Like many good mothers, Salome wanted the very best for her children. Good mothers pray for and encourage their children. They care for them well and provide for them well. They cook their favorite foods and cheer them on in their work and activities. They take great pride in watching them succeed. But good mothers must be careful because sometimes they focus too much on what they think is best for their children rather than what God knows is best.

Salome prayed to Jesus for a big blessing for her children, but Jesus didn't answer her prayer the way she hoped. Yet Salome still remained faithful and close to Jesus. She was one of the women looking on when Jesus died on the cross. How heartbroken she must have been! But she was also one of the first women to discover Jesus was alive again. And how happy she must have been then!

God greatly blesses the mothers who are faithful followers of Jesus, even when He doesn't always answer their prayers for their children the way they want or expect. You can help to be a blessing by being an obedient and respectful child. Children who please their parents please God!

(Adapted from Matthew 20)

JUNE

Celebration of Fathers

God gave men extraspecial strength and abilities to be great dads. The best kind of daddy is one who wants to be like our heavenly Father. Earthly dads cannot be perfect like our Father God, but they can strive to be full of His love, His goodness, and His wisdom. They can protect and provide for their children, like God protects and provides for His children. They can teach and share all they know and guide their children in good things. They can give the coolest rides on their shoulders and the biggest bear hugs too!

What a blessing good fathers are! At every time of year, hug yours—or someone who is like a father to you—tight, and tell him thank you for everything he does for you every chance you get. And especially during the month of June, when we have the holiday of Father's Day, we should appreciate, honor, and celebrate the good dads in our lives.

The Bible blesses us with wonderful examples of good fathers who loved their children well. We can learn from their lives and appreciate, honor, and celebrate them too. Read the following stories and see for yourself!

JESUS' EARTHLY FATHER

The Story of Joseph

Joseph never thought he was anyone special. He was a humble man who lived in a town called Nazareth. He worked as a carpenter and looked forward to marrying a lovely girl named Mary. He sure never expected to become a dad so fast. . .

Joseph and Mary were only engaged when she came to him and said she was pregnant through the Holy Spirit. What did that even mean? Joseph had never heard of such a thing! At first he was upset. Very much so. He would surely break up with Mary. Yet he still cared for her. Joseph was a man of integrity. He wanted to obey God and do the right thing. So he made a plan to break up with Mary quietly so he wouldn't publicly humiliate her.

But then an angel of the Lord appeared to Joseph in a dream and said, "Joseph, it's okay. Don't be afraid to take Mary as your wife. The baby growing inside her truly is from God. She will give birth to Him, and you must name Him Jesus because He will save His people from their sins."

When Joseph woke up, he obeyed what the angel of the Lord had said. He took Mary as his wife and cared for her with honor. When it was almost time for Mary to have her baby, the emperor of Rome decreed that Joseph and Mary must travel to Bethlehem to register in a census. What a nuisance for a young mom ready to give birth! Even worse—when they arrived in Bethlehem they couldn't find a place to stay. Yet Joseph kept calm and let God lead, and God used all these details to fulfill His promises. Joseph helped protect and provide for Mary until the time came that Jesus was born. And he continued protecting and providing for his wife and son as God guided, even running away to Egypt with them when evil King Herod wanted to have young Jesus killed.

After Herod died, an angel of the Lord came to Joseph again in a dream to tell him, "Go back to Israel. It's safe now. Those who wanted to kill Jesus are dead."

So Joseph obeyed and went back to Nazareth, just as God had planned for Jesus and directed through Joseph's dreams.

At first, in his anger and confusion, Joseph could have chosen to ignore the angel who told him to take Mary as his wife. Joseph could have taken the easy way out. But Joseph was a good man who unexpectedly became an even better man as an earthly father—because he listened with love to the heavenly Father.

(Adapted from Matthew 1–2)

~ FATHER OF THE WILDERNESS PREACHER ~

The Story of Zechariah

When the Jewish priest Zechariah was told by an angel of the Lord that his wife was going to have a son, he didn't believe his ears. Zechariah asked, "How is this possible? My wife and I are too old to have children!"

It was not good that Zechariah did not believe God's message. The angel said, "I am Gabriel. I stand in the presence of God and have been sent to tell you this good news. Now you will be unable to speak until your son is born because you did not believe my words, which will come true at just the right time."

And, just like the angel said would happen, suddenly Zechariah could not speak. He came out of the temple, and the people wondered what was wrong. What had taken so long? Why couldn't he talk to them? Zechariah kept making signs with his hands, and the people figured out that he'd seen something special in the temple.

Zechariah went home quietly, and Elizabeth did become pregnant. When it was time to have her baby, she gave birth to a son. All the family and friends assumed the baby would be named after his father, but Elizabeth said, "No! His name should be John." This was surprising because family names were so important. The people tried to talk to Zechariah. Surely he would not agree to Elizabeth's choice of name!

Zechariah, who still couldn't speak, asked for a writing tablet. He shocked everyone when he wrote down:

His name is John.

And in that moment of obeying God, he instantly gained his voice back. He began

to speak, praising God!

People all over the area heard of this miracle and were amazed and wondered about what a special child Zechariah and Elizabeth's son, John, must be. Indeed, he was extraordinary.

Zechariah was filled with the Holy Spirit and said to his new son, "You will be called a prophet of God, the Most High. You will go on before the Lord to prepare the way for Him, to tell people about salvation through forgiveness of sin."

Young John grew and became strong and went to live in the wilderness. Then one day God called him out of the wilderness to begin preaching about Jesus and preparing the way for Jesus.

(Adapted from Luke 1)

FATHER OF TWINS

The Story of Isaac

Isaac was the son born to Abraham and Sarah. His name meant "laughter." When Isaac grew up, he married Rebekah, whom he loved very much. When Isaac was sixty years old, Rebekah gave birth to two baby boys. The first baby to be born was all red and was covered with hair all over his body. His parents said, "We'll name him Esau." The second baby was holding on to baby Esau's heel as he was born. His parents said, "We'll name him Jacob." And Isaac was proud to be the father of twins.

The twin boys grew up and were very different from each other. Esau was a good hunter and loved to be outdoors. Jacob was quieter and loved to stay at home. Isaac's favorite son was Esau, and Rebekah's favorite son was Jacob.

One day, Jacob was at home cooking stew, and Esau came in from hunting outdoors. "I'm starving!" he said. "Jacob, give me some of that stew you're making."

And Jacob decided to be tricky. He said, "If you want my stew to eat, you have to give me your birthright. I want all of your rights as the firstborn son." Esau was so hungry he didn't care one bit about his rights as firstborn son. He just wanted to eat. So he promised to hand over his rights to Jacob, the younger son. Esau didn't think it was any big deal. Then he ate some stew and bread and got up and left.

Years later, when Isaac was so old he could hardly see anymore, he called for Esau to come to him. Isaac said, "Esau, I'm old and don't know how much longer I have to live. Go hunt some wild meat for me and cook me the tasty food I like. Then bring it to me to eat, and I will give you my blessing before I die."

Rebekah was still playing favorites. She overheard all this but wanted Jacob to get Isaac's blessing. While Esau was gone, she went to Jacob to make a quick plan to trick Isaac. She said to Jacob, "Go get two goats, and I will cook the food your father likes. Put on your brother's clothes, and put on goat hair to cover your skin. You will seem just like Esau to your father who cannot see."

So Jacob did as his mother told him, and together they tricked Isaac. He gave the blessing of the firstborn son to Jacob instead of Esau. When Isaac discovered what had happened, he was upset that he'd been tricked.

Isaac and Rebekah dearly loved their twin sons, but playing favorites and being dishonest caused great trouble in their family. Still, through Isaac's faithfulness and his family, God was working out His plans for His people.

(Adapted from Genesis 25:19–34; 27:1–40)

A PLEA FOR A SON'S HEALING

The Story of the Nobleman

During the time of Jesus' travels and ministry, He went again to Cana in Galilee. It was the same place He had done His first miracle—turning water into wine. While Jesus was there, a man from the town of Capernaum came to see Him. This man was a nobleman, a royal official who worked for the king, and he had government authority over Jesus. But he had heard a lot about Jesus and respected Him. The nobleman came to Jesus and said, "Sir, please come to my son! He is sick. I'm begging You to heal him. Please, *please* come to him before he dies!"

And Jesus said to him, "You may go. Your son will live."

But that's not exactly what the nobleman wanted to hear! Surely Jesus needed to actually be with his son to heal him. The nobleman had urged Jesus to come to Capernaum where his son was home in bed. And with his authority, the nobleman could have ordered Jesus to do so. So, he had to decide: Should he trust that Jesus could heal simply by saying the words from afar? Yes, the nobleman concluded. He believed Jesus had the power to miraculously heal, and he trusted Jesus would do it. He took Jesus at His word and left Cana.

The nobleman headed back to his home in Capernaum, about twenty miles away. He was anxious and eager to get back to his son. While he was still traveling, some of his servants met him along the way.

"Your son!" they cried. "He is alive!"

The nobleman was filled with joy and relief! Then he asked, "What time did he get better?"

The servants said, "His fever left him yesterday at the seventh hour."

Aha! The father realized that was the *exact* time that Jesus had said to him, "Your son will live."

From then on, not only did the nobleman believe in Jesus but so did everyone in his household. Because of the faith of a good father, many more were saved for believing in Jesus Christ.

(Adapted from John 4:46–54)

Prayers of Fathers

In June, the month of Father's Day, we honor and celebrate our dads and those who are like fathers to us. We give them presents and make them treats; we hug them tight and kiss their cheeks! We let them know what a blessing they are to us and tell them all the things we appreciate about them. We should especially appreciate a dad who prays! A loving dad who prays for his children is an extraspecial treasure. His prayers are so heartfelt and important. He wants the very best for his children, and he prays to God to ask for His blessings and protection and good gifts for them. He loves to take care of his children, but he knows that sometimes he can't. He also knows that it's ultimately God who takes care of them in all things. We can learn from what God's Word shares with us about Bible-time fathers and their prayers for their children. Read the following stories and see for yourself!

"PUT YOUR HAND ON HER THAT SHE MAY BE HEALED"

Jairus' Prayer for His Daughter

Jairus was an important Jewish man, a religious ruler in the synagogue of Capernaum. He was also a father to a beloved daughter. When the girl was twelve years old, she grew very, very sick—maybe with a fiery fever or an awful skin disease. Whatever her illness was, we know that she was much loved by her father and mother and others.

One day when Jesus was near the seashore, surrounded by a crowd of people, Jairus came and got down on his knees before Him. He cried out, saying, "My daughter is almost dead. Please come and put Your hand on her that she may be healed and live." So Jesus went with Jairus.

Everywhere Jesus went, there were miracles. Another one happened on the way to Jairus' house! In the crowd following Jesus was a woman who had been sick for twelve years with bleeding that would not stop. She had gone to many doctors and spent all her money trying to get better. But she had only gotten worse. Still, she had hope. This woman had heard about Jesus and had come to see Him. And then she simply touched His coat. For she said to herself, "If I can only touch His coat, I will be healed." At the very moment she touched Jesus' coat, her bleeding stopped! She felt in her body that she was healed of her sickness. How powerful Jesus is! No wonder Jairus wanted Jesus to come to his daughter. Jairus believed Jesus could simply put His hand on his daughter and she would live. And Jairus was right.

Jesus told Jairus not to be afraid but to believe, and once he got to Jairus' home, He went to the room where the daughter lay. Jesus told the many people crying for her that she was only sleeping. But it was clear to them that the young girl had died. Then Jesus told everyone except Jairus and his wife to leave the room. He took their daughter by the hand and said, "Little girl, get up!" Right away, she got up, good as new! Do you think she danced and jumped around as she celebrated with her mom and dad?

Even in his high position, Jairus was not full of pride. Instead, he was willing to go to Jesus humbly and ask for help. That's something all of us should do.

(Adapted from Matthew 9; Mark 5; Luke 8)

"LORD, HAVE PITY ON MY SON!"

A Father's Prayer for His Demon-Possessed Boy

One day a father got down on his knees before Jesus. He prayed, "Lord, have pity on my son. Please help him! A demon takes him and won't let him talk. The demon takes hold of him and makes him shake. Spit runs from his mouth, and he grinds his teeth. Wherever the demon takes him, it throws him down. The demon won't leave, and my son is getting weaker."

The poor father's heart broke for his son. He was very troubled because he didn't know what to do. He had asked the disciples to cast out the demon, but they could not. Still, he had hope.

Jesus said, "Bring your son to Me."

So they brought the boy to Jesus. The demon saw Jesus and at once held the boy in its power. The boy fell to the ground with spit running from his mouth. Then Jesus asked, "How long has he been like this?"

The father said, "He's been like this since he was a tiny boy. Many times, the demon throws him into the fire and into the water to kill him. If You can do anything to help us, take pity on us!"

Jesus said to him, "Why do you say *if* I can? The one who has faith can do all things."

At once the father cried out with tears in his eyes, "Lord, I have faith. Help my weak faith to be stronger!"

Jesus spoke sharp words to the demon. He said, "Come out of him! Do not ever go into him again." The demon gave a cry. It threw the boy down and came out of him. The boy was so still and lifeless at first that the people said, "He is dead!" But Jesus took the boy by the hand and helped him up. Then Jesus gave the boy back to his grateful father.

Later the disciples came to Jesus when He was alone. They asked, "Why were we not able to put the demon out?" Jesus said to them, "Because you have so little faith. I tell you, if you only have faith as small as a mustard seed, you could say to this mountain, 'Move from here to over there,' and it would move over. You will be able to do anything."

All we need is a little faith and we can move mountains too!

(Adapted from Matthew 17; Mark 9)

"PLEASE COME TO CAPERNAUM!"

The Royal Official's Prayer for His Dying Son

Jesus' first miracle on earth was in the town of Cana in Galilee. One day as He was traveling, Jesus returned to Cana. While He was there, an official who worked with the king came to Jesus. The royal official had traveled over twenty miles to Cana—all the way from Capernaum—to meet Jesus and ask Him to help the official's son, who was very sick.

When the official came to Jesus, he asked, "Will You please come to Capernaum to heal my son who is dying?"

Jesus replied, "Unless you see special things and powerful works done, you will not believe."

The royal official said, "Sir, please come with me before my son dies."

But Jesus decided not to go with him. He simply said, "Go on your way. Your son will live."

The royal official put his trust in what Jesus said. He could have been angry and bitter that Jesus did not do exactly as he'd asked. He could have begged Jesus to actually come to his house so that Jesus could put His healing hand on the boy. Instead, the official chose to believe that even from miles away, Jesus had all power to heal.

So the royal official left to make his way home again to Capernaum, believing and trusting in Jesus' promise. As he was on his way, his servants met him along the road. "Your son!" they exclaimed. "He is living!"

Relief and gratitude filled the royal official. "When was it?" he asked. "What time did

my son begin to get well?"

They answered, "Yesterday at one o'clock."

The father was amazed, and his faith in Jesus grew, because he knew one o'clock was the exact time Jesus had said to him, "Your son will live."

What a happy reunion for father and son when the royal official got home. Then he and everyone in his house put their trust in Jesus.

(Adapted from John 4:46–54)

"LORD, WHAT WILL YOU GIVE ME? FOR I HAVE NO CHILD"

Abraham's Prayer for an Heir

Abraham was one of God's special people, and he was called a friend of God. As the years were passing and he was growing older and older, he prayed to God to give him a son, for he had none. In those days, it was the custom that the oldest servant of the household would be the heir of any man who had no son. While Abraham respected and trusted his servant Eliezer, he still longed to have a son of his own. Abraham prayed, "Lord, what will You give me? For I have no child. And the one who is to receive what belongs to me is Eliezer. Because You have not given me a child, he is the one who will be given all I have."

Then the word of the Lord came to him, saying, "Your servant Eliezer will not be given what is yours. But a son who will come from you will be given what is yours."

Then God took Abraham outside and said, "Now look up into the heavens and add up the stars, if you are able to count them." God knew it was impossible for any human to do! But God said to Abraham, "Your children and your children's children will be as many as the stars."

Abraham must have been amazed by this. An old man with no children would have as many descendants as the stars in the night sky? He must have thought, *Impossible!* But everything is possible with God. Hard to believe? Yes! Abraham could have laughed at God's words. But he believed in the Lord, and that made him right with God. Abraham

trusted God, and so he was considered righteous.

God's promises are always true, even when He takes His time in making them happen. The promised son, Isaac, was born when Abraham was one hundred years old and Sarah was ninety! Isaac's name means "laughter." His mom, Sarah, had laughed in disbelief when God said she would have a son in her old age. But God had responded, "Is anything too hard for the Lord?"

Abraham, a faithful, praying father, knew the answer to that question was, "Surely not!"

(Adapted from Genesis 15; 18; 21)

JULY

Freedom!

What makes you feel free? Is it the sound of the final bell ringing on the last day of school before break? Is it when you wake up on a Saturday morning with no alarms and no plans, and you have all day to play whatever you want? Is it appreciating freedom in our nation and celebrating the Fourth of July with your family?

Maybe you've been trapped in an awful situation and you felt the great relief of freedom when someone helped you out. Jesus offers that kind of help and that kind of freedom. Every person is born into this world trapped in sin, trapped in the bad things we think and do without even trying—like how selfish thoughts pop up in our minds without us wanting them to. But because Jesus suffered and died on the cross to take the punishment for our sins, we can accept His gift of salvation and be totally free from sin forever. Then we will rise again when we die like He did and have eternal life like He does. That is true freedom forever!

In a world that is full of hard things, we sometimes find ourselves feeling trapped in difficult situations, but God offers help and hope for those things too. The Bible gives us wonderful true stories of times when God rescued and freed His people. We can trust in these stories and find encouragement and hope for ourselves today. Read the following stories and see for yourself!

THE LIONS' DEN

The Story of Daniel

When King Nebuchadnezzar of Babylon came to Jerusalem and captured it to be under his rule, he ordered some of the brightest and strongest Israelite men be brought to his palace. He wanted them to train in the ways of the Babylonians so they could one day serve the king. Daniel was one of these smart and strong young men. Daniel also wanted to stay faithful to the one true God, and God blessed him for that. King Nebuchadnezzar respected Daniel and gave him important jobs and many gifts.

Time passed, and a new king came to power in Babylon—King Darius. And still Daniel was one of the most respected leaders in the land. All was well for Daniel until some leaders under him became jealous. They wanted to find a way to get Daniel in trouble with the king. But the bad men could find nothing to accuse Daniel of. So they came up with an evil plan.

The jealous leaders went to King Darius and said, "King, you should make a law saying that for the next thirty days, no one in the kingdom is allowed to pray to anyone but you. If they do, they will be thrown into the den of lions!" King Darius agreed and put out a written decree that everyone in the kingdom must obey this new law.

But Daniel loved the one true God and would never stop praying to Him alone. Despite the new law, he continued to pray to the Lord and not to King Darius. Three times a day he prayed to God in front of his open window. The jealous leaders had been hoping for this. They quickly went to the king to report what Daniel was doing.

"Daniel is paying no attention to you or this law," the jealous leaders tattled.

King Darius was greatly troubled, because he liked and respected Daniel. But the jealous leaders convinced the king to follow through with the law. So the king gave the order, and Daniel was thrown into the den of lions. The king said to Daniel, "May your God, whom you serve faithfully, rescue you!" Then the den was closed up tight.

King Darius could not eat that evening or sleep that night. He felt awful. First thing in the morning, he hurried to the den of lions and called out, "Daniel, servant of the living God, has your God been able to save you from the lions?"

And Daniel answered! "My God sent His angel and shut the mouths of the lions. He knows I am not guilty. I have done nothing wrong before you either, O king."

With great joy, the king ordered Daniel out of the lions' den. There was not even a single scratch on Daniel!

And soon King Darius decreed, "In every part of my kingdom, people must respect and honor the God of Daniel. He is the living God forever. He rescues and saves. He has freed Daniel from the power of the lions."

(Adapted from Daniel 1; 6)

THE PARTING OF THE RED SEA

The Story of Moses

God's people were tired of being slaves. For years they'd been treated cruelly under Pharaoh's power. Moses was an Israelite who had grown up in Pharaoh's palace because the princess had rescued Moses from the Nile River when he was a baby. But as a young man, Moses had run away to another country. Then God called Moses back to Egypt to lead the Israelites out of slavery and into freedom.

Moses had a lot of fear and many questions about the task God had given him, so God sent Moses' brother, Aaron, to help. God also gave Moses a shepherd's staff to perform incredible miracles.

Moses and Aaron went to Pharaoh and told him that the Lord God of Israel said, "Let My people go!" But Pharaoh refused and was even crueler to the Israelites, beating them and calling them lazy and making their work harder to do.

God guided Moses and Aaron to keep telling Pharaoh, "Let the Israelites go." And still, Pharaoh would not listen.

Then God told Moses and Aaron to use the special staff He had given them to bring plagues on the Egyptian people as punishment for keeping the Israelites in slavery. Moses and Aaron obeyed. Surely these plagues would make Pharaoh listen and free the Israelites.

First God turned the Nile River to blood so that all the fish died and no one could drink the water.

Still Pharaoh would not listen.

God also sent frogs and gnats and flies and killed all of Egypt's livestock. Still

Pharaoh would not listen.

Then God sent boils and hail and locusts and total darkness on the land. Still Pharaoh would not listen.

Then God vowed to kill every firstborn son in all of Egypt because Pharaoh refused to free the Israelites. But He made a way to protect the firstborn sons of Israel. And just as God said it would happen, all firstborn sons of Egypt died, but all firstborn sons of Israel were safe. Finally Pharaoh listened and let God's people go.

As they fled from Egypt, God led the Israelites with a huge cloud in the sky during the day and fire in the sky at night. Meanwhile back in Egypt, Pharaoh changed his mind and sent his armies out to capture the Israelites again. The Egyptians caught up with the Israelites at the Red Sea, and God's people seemed to be trapped. God, however, had an amazing plan. Moses stretched his hand toward the sea, and God drove the waters back and made a path of dry land through the Red Sea! The Israelites followed the path with huge walls of water rising up on either side of them. As the Egyptians chased the Israelites, God made the waters crash down to kill the Egyptians, but He kept the Israelites safe.

Just as He had promised, God made a miraculous way to bring His people out of slavery and into freedom.

(Adapted from Exodus 1–14)

A JAILER IS SAVED

The Story of Paul and Silas

After God changed Paul's heart on the road to Damascus, Paul preached the good news of Jesus Christ to many people. He traveled all over, performing miracles through God's power and helping many to trust in Jesus as their Savior. On one of his travels, his friend Silas was with him, and the two friends met a slave girl who had an evil spirit within her. With this evil spirit the girl predicted the future, which people were willing to pay lots of money for. So the girl was making her owners rich.

The evil spirit inside the girl also wanted to bother Paul and Silas. So the girl followed them, taunting and teasing them day after day. Finally, Paul was so troubled by this that he turned to the girl and said to the evil spirit within her, "In the name of Jesus Christ, I command you to come out of her." And at that moment the evil spirit left her.

The slave girl's owners were furious! Now they would make no more money from the girl. They captured Paul and Silas and dragged them to the town leaders and accused them of causing trouble in their town. The leaders ordered Paul and Silas to be stripped and beaten and thrown in jail. The prison guards were told to watch them carefully so they could not escape. They were put in the inner jail cell and had their feet chained up too.

None of this stopped Paul's and Silas' faith in God. Late that night, they were praying and singing to God, and other prisoners were listening to them. Suddenly an earthquake shook the jail. It was so strong that the prison doors flew open and everyone's chains broke loose.

The jailer woke up and was terrified. He thought he would be killed for all the prisoners going free.

But Paul said to him, "We are all here!" And the jailer ran to Paul and Silas and dropped to the ground in front of them. Then he brought them out of their jail cell and said, "What should I do to be saved?"

They told him, "Believe in the Lord Jesus, and you will be saved. You and your household."

And then the jailer took Paul and Silas to his home and cared for them and fed them a meal. And everyone in his family listened to Paul and Silas and believed in Jesus. The jailer and his family were filled with joy that night. Even more amazing than freedom from a prison cell, they had found forever freedom in Jesus Christ.

(Adapted from Acts 16:16–40)

THE COURAGEOUS DREAMER

The Story of Joseph

Joseph was a young Israelite man who was dearly loved by his father, Jacob. He had ten older brothers and one younger. The brothers were jealous and hateful toward Joseph. When their father gave Joseph a special robe made of many colors and designs, they grew even more jealous. And when Joseph told his brothers his dreams, they grew even more hateful.

Joseph said to them, "Listen, I had a dream that we were gathering grain in the field. My bundle of grain stood up, and all of your bundles of grain bowed down to mine."

His brothers said, "Do you think this means you're going to be our king and rule over us?" And they hated Joseph all the more.

Then Joseph told them another dream: "Listen, this time in my dream the sun and moon and eleven stars were bowing down to me."

The hateful brothers couldn't stand it. They made evil plans against Joseph and finally sold him to traveling merchants who took him to Egypt to be a slave. They tricked their father into thinking Joseph had been killed by a wild animal.

In Egypt, Joseph worked for Potiphar, who was the captain of the guard for the king. God was with Joseph, and he succeeded at everything he did. Potiphar greatly respected and trusted Joseph and put him in charge of everything he owned. But then Potiphar's wife was cruel to Joseph and tricked her husband into thinking Joseph was bad. So Joseph was put in prison.

Still God was with Joseph, and he found favor with the jailer. Soon Joseph was in

charge of all the other prisoners. God also gave Joseph the ability to understand dreams, and Joseph helped fellow prisoners interpret theirs.

One day Pharaoh called for Joseph to be brought out of prison. Pharaoh said to Joseph, "I have had a dream that no one else can interpret. I've heard that you can do it."

Joseph replied, "I cannot do it, but God can." And with God's help, Joseph told Pharaoh what his dreams meant. The dreams revealed how Egypt could survive a great coming famine that would cause the people to starve and ruin their kingdom if they did not plan ahead.

Pharaoh was so grateful that he called Joseph the wisest in the land. Then he put Joseph in a high position over all the people.

God had surely worked His good ways through Joseph! He brought Joseph out of slavery and prison and into freedom and great power and blessing in the land of Egypt.

(Adapted from Genesis 37; 39–41)

Prayers for Forgiveness

In July, people in the United States celebrate the freedom of America with flags and fireworks and family picnics. It's all so much fun! But you can celebrate an even better freedom in your heart all year long. You can have spiritual freedom because Jesus can forgive us from the sins (the bad things we say and think and do) that trap us. You know how good it feels to tell someone you're sorry after you've done something wrong and to hear them say it's okay, so you know forgiveness is a wonderful gift! When we admit our sins to Jesus and tell Him we're sorry and that we need Him to be our Savior, He forgives all our sins forever. That's such a huge relief because we all make mistakes and bad choices sometimes. And because Jesus forgives us so well, we should want to do our best to keep away from sin and forgive others too. The stories in the Bible of times when people prayed to God for forgiveness help us learn why it's so important. Read the following stories and see for yourself!

"TAKE AWAY THE SNAKES"

Moses' Prayer for Forgiveness for the Israelites

Do you remember how God's people, the Israelites, were slaves in Egypt? But then God sent plagues—like the bloody river, frogs and flies, skin sores and hail and locusts, and finally death—across the land of Egypt until Pharaoh finally agreed to let God's people go. Then God used Moses to lead His people out of Egypt, and they wandered in the desert for many years. Remember how they grumbled and complained and made God angry, especially when they made a golden calf to worship? But God forgave them when Moses prayed on their behalf.

After many years of wandering in the wilderness and hoping to settle in the Promised Land, one day they were feeling crabby again. And they were grumbling again. They spoke against God and Moses, saying, "Why have you brought us out of Egypt to die in the desert? There is no food and no water."

God was not pleased with their bad attitudes and complaints. He was very upset with their behavior, and they were in big trouble. So He punished them to teach them a lesson. These were no ordinary consequences—not just going to bed early or doing extra chores or missing out on something fun. No, God sent poisonous snakes! Mean and nasty snakes. The snakes bit the people, and many of the people died. It was a horrible and scary time, and many of the Israelites wished they had never grumbled and complained. They were very sorry for their sins. They came to Moses and said, "We have sinned by speaking against the Lord and you. Please pray to the Lord. Please pray that He will take away the snakes from us."

Then Moses prayed that God would forgive the Israelites and take away the snakes. And God listened and answered Moses with specific instructions. "Make a special snake and put it up on a long wooden pole. Everyone who is bitten will live when they look at it." So Moses made a brass snake and put it at the top of a long piece of wood. If a snake bit anyone, they would live when they looked at the brass snake.

Once again, God showed His great love and mercy for His people even when they sinned against Him. He was willing to forgive them when they humbled themselves and admitted they had done wrong. God's perfect forgiveness freed them from the fear of the snakes and the guilty weight of their sins.

(Adapted from Numbers 21:4–9)

"O LORD, HEAR! O LORD, FORGIVE!"

Daniel's Prayer for Forgiveness of Israel's Sins

Do you remember how God rescued Daniel from the lions' den? That same Daniel often had incredible visions and dreams, and he prayed heartfelt prayers. One day he begged God to remember His promise to return the Israelites to their land.

Daniel prayed to God and did not eat. He wore uncomfortable clothes and covered himself with ashes. First he praised God, saying, "Lord, You are great, and we fear You. You keep Your promises and show loving-kindness to those who love You."

Then Daniel confessed the sins of the people. He prayed, "We have done wrong. We have turned against You. We have not listened to Your servants who spoke for You. You are right and good, O Lord. But we are all covered with shame because we have not been faithful to You. But, Lord, You are kind and forgiving, even though we've disobeyed You. We've earned the curses and punishments that You have poured out on us, which were written about in the Law of God's servant Moses. God has done what He said He would do against us and our leaders and has brought much trouble on us. Yet we have not looked for the favor of the Lord our God by turning from our sin and following Your truth."

And then Daniel asked God for His forgiveness and goodness and blessing, saying, "O Lord, because You are right and good in what You do, do not be angry any longer with Your city Jerusalem. For because of our sins and the sins of our fathers, Jerusalem and Your people have been put to shame by everyone around us. So now, our God, please listen to my prayer. Look with favor on the house of God that now lies in waste. Please, God, open Your eyes and see our trouble. We are not asking this of You because we are right or good but because of Your great loving-pity. O Lord, hear! O Lord, forgive! O Lord, listen and act! For Your glory, God, do not wait. Because Your city and Your people are called by Your name."

Daniel's prayer shows us what it means to be faithful to God. He taught us how to pray with praise and confession and humble requests to receive God's forgiveness.

(Adapted from Daniel 9)

"FATHER, FORGIVE THEM!"

Jesus' Prayer for the People Crucifying Him

Near the end of Jesus' life on earth, He predicted what would happen before He died. And all those things started to come true. His friend Judas helped soldiers find and capture Jesus in exchange for thirty pieces of silver. Then those soldiers took Jesus to the Jewish leaders who hated Him. They accused Jesus of bad things He'd never done! From there, Jesus was taken to the palace of Pilate, the Roman governor. Pilate did not believe in Jesus, but he didn't want to kill Him either. "I find nothing wrong in this Man," Pilate said. But he handed Jesus over to His enemies. They spit on Jesus and put a painful crown of sharp thorns on His head. They mocked Him and taunted Him and beat Him up.

Pilate tried again to free Jesus. He called together the people who wanted to kill Jesus and said, "You brought this Man to me as one who leads the people in the wrong way, but I do not find Him guilty of the things you say. King Herod found nothing wrong with Him either, because he sent Him back to us. There is no reason to have Him put to death. I will punish Him and let Him go free."

But the Jewish people who hated Jesus insisted that He should die. They even demanded that Barabbas, a man who had killed people and caused all kinds of trouble, go free instead of Jesus. They yelled out, "Nail Jesus to a cross!" Over and over they shouted, "Crucify Him! Crucify Him!"

So Pilate said to them a third time, "Why? What bad thing has He done? I have found no reason to put Him to death."

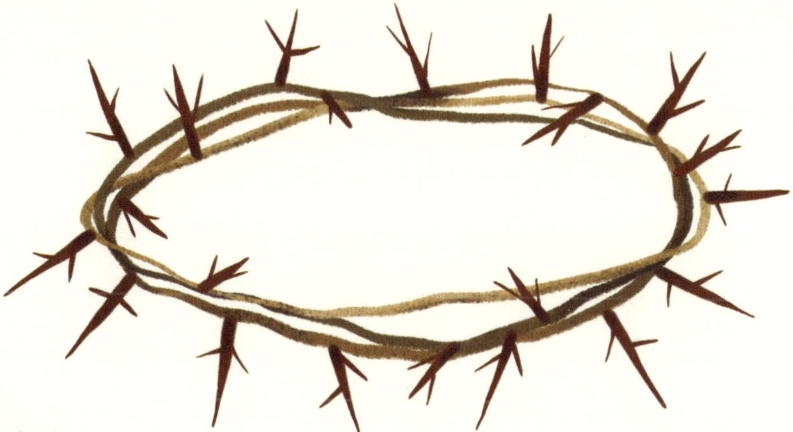

But they kept shouting and yelling that He must be killed. And finally, Pilate gave in. He let Barabbas go free and he gave Jesus over to the angry crowd.

Jesus had done nothing wrong, but the people who hated Him were cruel and unfair. But even as He was being put to death, working out God's plan for salvation that would be for all people, Jesus loved the people who hated Him. He cried out from the cross in prayer as He suffered. He said, "Father, forgive them! They do not know what they are doing."

No one else has ever had such amazing love and forgiveness for people as Jesus Christ. He suffered and died to take away sin and free all who trust in Him as Savior.

(Adapted from Luke 22–23; John 19)

"LORD, DO NOT HOLD THIS SIN AGAINST THEM"

Stephen's Prayer for His Killers

After Jesus died on the cross, He rose again and went up to heaven. Then God's Holy Spirit came to live inside Jesus' followers. As more and more people became believers, Jesus' church grew. Church leaders chose helpers to care for people in need. Stephen was chosen to help give out food.

Stephen was a Christian who was full of faith and power. He spoke with the wisdom of the Holy Spirit. But some of the religious leaders who had hated Jesus hated Stephen too. "We have heard him say things against Moses and God," they said. In this way they got the people talking against Stephen. They took him to the religious leaders' court where people lied about him. But even though people were trying to get him in trouble, Stephen was strong and calm and full of peace. His face even looked like the face of an angel!

The head religious leader asked Stephen, "Are these things true?"

Stephen didn't even try to defend himself. He was mostly concerned about saying what God wanted him to share. So he preached a message about the history of Israel and the nation's relationship with God. Stephen boldly told the religious leaders they were wrong to reject and kill Jesus. The final words of his message were, "You have hard hearts and ears that will not listen to me! You are always working against the Holy Spirit. Your early fathers did too. They killed those who told of the coming of Jesus. Now you have handed Him over and killed Him. You had the Law given to you by angels. Yet you have not kept it."

When Stephen finished speaking, the religious leaders in the court were furious. But Stephen was filled with the Holy Spirit. As he looked up to heaven, he saw the shining-greatness of God and Jesus. He said, "I see heaven open and the Son of Man standing at the right side of God!"

The religious leaders grew even angrier. They grabbed Stephen, dragged him out of the city, and began to throw stones at him to kill him.

Stephen knew he would soon die. But even as he suffered, he fell on his knees and prayed for the people killing him. Stephen cried out in a loud voice, "Lord, do not hold this sin against them."

True forgiveness means we don't hold sin against anyone. We set them free from our desire to pay them back—no matter how awfully they behaved. Since we've been forgiven by Jesus, we can offer forgiveness to others like Stephen did.

(Adapted from Acts 6–7)

AUGUST

Learning and Wisdom

The end of summer brings back-to-school time and all the excitement (maybe some jitters too!) of a new year of learning. God's Word says, "The fear of the LORD is the beginning of wisdom" (Proverbs 9:10 NIV). But that doesn't mean we need to be scared of God. It means we should honor and respect God as the Creator of everything. Believing in and worshipping Him are where we start to have knowledge and wisdom about anything and everything.

In God's Word, there are endless things for us to learn and apply to our lives so that we may grow closer in relationship with God. All the writing in the Bible is God-given and made alive by Him. We get help when we are taught God's Word. It shows us what is wrong. It changes the way of our lives. It shows us how to be right with God. It gives those of us who belong to God everything we need to work well for Him (2 Timothy 3:16–17). The Bible should be our first source of learning, and we should filter everything we learn about the world through it—keeping the good and getting rid of the bad.

God's Word gives many examples of how real people listened and learned and gained wisdom. We can study the stories of their lives and apply what they learned to our own lives. Read the following stories and see for yourself!

A PRAYER FOR WISDOM

The Story of Solomon

When King David of Israel grew old and knew he would soon die, he said to his son Solomon, "Be strong and do what the Lord your God tells you. Walk in His ways. Keep all of His laws and His Word. Then you will succeed in all that you do and in every place you go." And when David died, Solomon ascended the throne and became the new king of Israel.

King Solomon did love God, and he walked in God's ways. One night, God appeared to him in a dream and said, "Ask Me for anything you want Me to give you."

Truly, anything? What an honor for King Solomon! He replied to God, "You were very kind to my father David because he was faithful and good and pure in heart before You. Now You have made me, Your servant, king in place of my father. But I'm just like a child. I don't know how to do things best, and there are so many people to rule over. So please give me wisdom and an understanding heart to judge Your people and know the difference between good and bad."

God was very happy that Solomon asked for this. God said to him, "You did not ask for a long life for yourself. You did not ask for riches or for your enemies to be defeated. But you have asked for understanding to know what is right. Because you have asked this, I have done what you asked. See, I have given you a wise and understanding heart. No one has been like you before, and there will be no one like you in the future. Plus I'm also giving you what you didn't ask for. I give you both riches and honor. There will be no other king like you all your days. And if you walk in My ways and keep My laws and

Word as your father did, I will allow you to live for a very long time."

Solomon woke from the dream and returned to Jerusalem. He praised and worshipped God and hosted a great feast for all of his servants.

King Solomon did not rule Israel perfectly, but he did his best to rule wisely. He continued to listen to and learn from God as he used the understanding he had asked for.

(Adapted from 1 Kings 2–3)

WHEN GOD SAYS, "GO"

The Story of Jonah

One day, God said to a man named Jonah, "Go to the big city of Nineveh to preach against it. The people there are very wicked. Tell them I have seen their terrible sins, and I am sending My judgment."

This was the last thing Jonah wanted to hear from God. He didn't want to go to Nineveh. He'd heard about how bad it was there, and he wanted nothing to do with that city or its people. So Jonah made his own travel plan. He tried to run away from God. He went to the town of Joppa and got on a boat setting sail for Tarshish.

God still wanted Jonah in Nineveh, so He caused a strong wind and a big storm on the seas where Jonah was sailing for Tarshish. The storm was so dangerous that Jonah's boat was about to break up in the waters. All the sailors were scared, and they were throwing heavy things off the boat to help it survive the storm. When they realized Jonah was below deck, they said to him, "How can you sleep? Get up and pray and maybe your God will save us!"

Then the sailors decided to draw names, trying to figure out who might have caused the storm. The name they drew was Jonah's. He explained to them that he was running away from God. "You'd better throw me into the sea," he said. "Then the seas will calm down. I know this bad storm has happened because of me."

But the sailors didn't want to throw Jonah overboard—if they did, he could be killed! They tried hard to row to shore but couldn't. So they prayed to God for mercy and then threw Jonah into the sea. Suddenly the storm stopped just like Jonah said it would.

Then the sailors worshipped the one true God and promised to serve Him.

And God still had plans for Jonah—weird ones! Jonah did not die in the storm or the seas. God sent a big fish to swallow him. It didn't hurt him. He simply sat in the stomach of that fish for three days and three nights. While he sat, he prayed and worshipped God. And then God told the fish to spit Jonah out onto dry land.

Once again, God told Jonah to get up and go to Nineveh to preach to the people there. Jonah had learned his lesson not to disobey God. He did not run away this time. He went to Nineveh and preached as God directed, and because the people listened and turned away from their sin, God saved their city from destruction.

(Adapted from Jonah 1–3)

THE WIFE OF A VERY FOOLISH MAN

The Story of Abigail

Not long before David became king of Israel, there was a man named Nabal who was very rich. He had three thousand sheep and one thousand goats. His wife's name was Abigail, and she was beautiful, kind, and wise. Nabal, on the other hand, was very foolish and sinful in all his ways.

David knew of Nabal and had helped protect the men who worked for him. He heard that Nabal was shearing sheep in a place called Carmel near where David and his men had set up camp. So David told some of his men to go to Nabal and ask him for food and supplies. David had been kind to Nabal's men, and he figured Nabal would be kind in return.

But Nabal simply scoffed at David's men. He didn't care that David was a powerful leader who had helped Nabal's men. He refused to share anything. When the men reported all this to David, he was extremely angry and told them, "Put on your swords!" He was ready to go fight and kill.

One of Nabal's men went to Abigail to inform her of what had happened. Then he warned her, "Beware and think about what you should do because David is very angry. Nabal is such a sinful man that no one can speak to him."

Right away, Abigail took two hundred loaves of bread, two bottles of wine, five sheep ready to eat, five baskets of dry grain, one hundred vines of dried grapes, and two hundred loaves of figs, and she loaded them on donkeys. Then she said to her men, "Take all this and go on ahead of me. I'll be right behind you." She did not tell her husband, Nabal.

As David and his men came down toward her, Abigail met them. David said to her, "I have been good to Nabal and his men, and he has been bad to me in return. By morning I will kill him and all his men."

Abigail fell at David's feet and said, "Listen to me, please, I beg you. Do not even think about this sinful man, Nabal. He is very foolish. Please let the Lord keep you from killing Nabal and his men. And let those who hate you and those who want to hurt you be foolish like Nabal."

David said to Abigail, "Thanks be to the Lord God of Israel for sending you to me. Thank you for your wisdom. You have kept me from being guilty of killing and from punishing with my own hand. Go up to your house in peace. I have listened to you and have done what you asked."

Nabal acted in foolishness and David nearly overreacted in great anger. But Abigail acted in generosity and wisdom and saved many lives.

(Adapted from 1 Samuel 25)

SPIES IN THE LAND

The Story of Joshua and Caleb

One day after the Israelites had escaped from slavery in Egypt and were wandering in the desert, God said to Moses, "Send some men to explore the land of Canaan, which I am going to give to the Israelites." Two of those men were Joshua and Caleb, and there were ten others, each one from a different tribe of the people of Israel. Moses said to them, "Go be like spies in Canaan. Find out everything you can about what the land is like. Is it easy to grow food or not? Are there many trees and plants? Are the cities small or large? Are there many people there? Are they weak or strong?"

So Joshua, Caleb, and the ten other men went to spy on the land of Canaan for forty days. When they returned, they reported, "The land of Canaan is wonderful! It's flowing with milk and honey." They showed some of the good fruit of the land they had brought back. "But," they said, "the people there are very powerful, and the cities there are large and well protected."

Even so, Caleb spoke up and said, "We should go take over the land of Canaan. We can do it!"

But ten of the spies said, "No way! The people

of Canaan are too strong for us. We could never take their land from them." And then the ten spies spread such fear among the people of Israel about Canaan that the people rebelled and complained against their leaders Moses and Aaron.

Again, Joshua and Caleb tried to encourage the people about what they had seen in Canaan. "The land of Canaan is wonderful. If God is pleased with us, He will lead us there and give it to us. But we must not disobey God or be afraid of the people of Canaan. God is on our side. He will be with us."

But the people were so upset they talked about throwing stones at Caleb and Joshua to kill them! And God was very angry. He appeared at the Tent of Meeting to all the Israelites and said to Moses, "How long will these people not believe in Me, even after all the miracles they've seen Me do? I will punish and destroy them!"

Moses asked God for kindness and forgiveness for the Israelites, and God had mercy on them. Still, He said that the ten spies who did not believe He would give the Israelites the land of Canaan would never enter it, but Joshua and Caleb would enter it and be blessed.

Joshua and Caleb learned that God punished those who doubted Him. But God greatly rewards those who are wise enough to remain courageous and strong in their faith in God's promises.

(Adapted from Numbers 13–14)

Prayers for Victory in Battle

Imagine that you have to take a long walk on the hottest summer day in August. The sun beats down with no mercy, and there's not even a breeze to cool you a little. You just took your last sip of water, and you still have a mile to go. Ugh! It sure takes perseverance to make it through the worst days of summer. And it sure takes perseverance to make it through all kinds of other challenges too. We need God's help! We need Him to give us victory over the tough times and people and situations that come against us. In the Bible, we learn about people who prayed for God to give them victory over the tough battles they found themselves in. They can encourage and inspire us when we need victory over our battles too. Read the following stories and see for yourself!

"SUN AND MOON, STAND STILL!"

Joshua's Prayer for a Miracle

Joshua was a faithful and courageous man who became the leader of the people of Israel after Moses died.

One day, Joshua found himself facing several enemies who had teamed up together. The king of Jerusalem heard that Joshua had destroyed a city called Ai. He also heard that the people of Gibeon had made peace with Israel and were living among them. That made him very afraid—because Gibeon was a large city, and all its men were strong. So the king of Jerusalem sent word to four other kings. He said to them, "Come and help me. Let's go fight against Gibeon. For it has made peace with Joshua and the people of Israel." So the five kings gathered together with all their armies. And they went and set up their tents by Gibeon, ready to fight.

Then the men of Gibeon sent word to Joshua. "Don't leave us alone! Hurry and help us!" they said. "For all the kings who live in the hill country have gathered against us."

So Joshua gathered all his warriors and strong soldiers. The Lord said to Joshua, "Don't be afraid of them. For I have already helped you win this battle."

So Joshua snuck up on them by surprise after traveling all night. The Lord brought trouble and destruction on the kings and their armies in front of Israel, and they ran away! And while they ran, the Lord made large hailstones fall from heaven on them.

Then Joshua spoke to the Lord on that day and said, "Sun and moon, stand still!" He was asking God to stop the sun and moon—and God did it. The sun stood still and the moon stopped until the nation of Israel punished those who fought against them.

That's right—the sun stopped in the center of the sky! It did not hurry to go down for nearly a whole day. There had been no day like it ever before, and there has been no day like it since. The Lord listened to Joshua, and the Lord fought for Israel. Then Joshua and the Israelite army returned to their tents.

The Lord fought for Israel and helped them win. Then He showed His power as the one true God over all creation—all powerful even over the sun and moon! The Lord fights for us to help us win life's battles too. Just ask for His help.

(Adapted from Joshua 10)

"GIVE ME STRENGTH ONCE MORE!"

Samson's Prayer to Defeat the Philistines

God gave Samson's mother and father special rules for his life even before the boy was born. An angel of the Lord told Samson's mom, "You will soon give birth to a son. His hair must never be cut. He will be dedicated to God from birth. He will begin to rescue Israel from the Philistines." She named the baby Samson, and God blessed him as he grew up.

God gave Samson incredible strength. One day as he was traveling, a lion attacked Samson. But the Spirit of the Lord powerfully filled Samson. He ripped the lion's jaws apart with his bare hands as if the lion were a baby goat!

Throughout his life, Samson fought with the Philistines. And the Philistines wondered how one man could have such incredible strength. One day some Philistine rulers came to Samson's girlfriend, Delilah. They promised to give her lots of money if she could trick Samson into sharing the secret of his great strength so they could know how to beat him. Delilah agreed to the plan.

At first, Samson would only tease Delilah when she asked him to share the truth about his strength. But after she begged and nagged Samson for days, he finally told her, "My hair has never been cut because I have been set apart for God since the day I was born. If my head were shaved, my strength would leave me." Delilah then lulled Samson to sleep on her lap and called a man in to cut off all Samson's hair.

When Samson woke up, at first he did not realize that the Lord had left him because his hair was cut. He tried to fight, but the Philistines captured him. They cut out his eyes and put him in prison.

Later on, the leaders of the Philistines gathered to make fun of Samson. They made him stand between the stone pillars that held up the temple they were in.

Samson's hair had grown again while he was in prison. Now he called out to God and said, "O Lord God, please remember me. Give me strength once more so that I can punish the Philistines." Then Samson took hold of the two pillars that held up the building. He pushed against them with all his strength so that the temple building fell. The Philistine leaders and thousands of Philistine people were killed. Samson died along with them, but God had worked out His plans through Samson—strong and powerful plans to free the Israelite people from the rule of the evil Philistines.

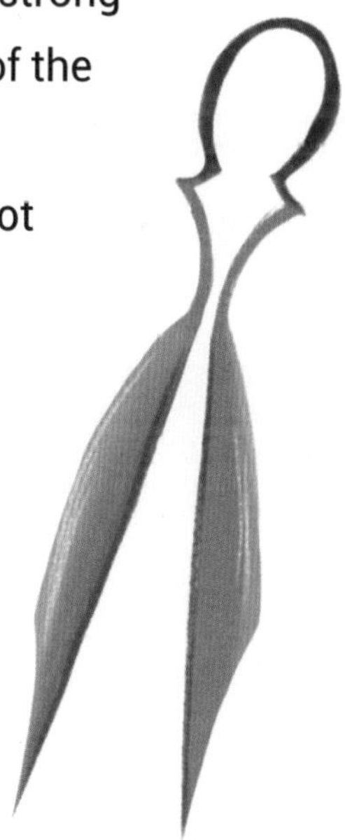

We too can pray to God for special strength. It might not be the power to knock down a building, but God will give us strength to get through all kinds of hard things. He will lead us to victory to bring about His good plans.

(Adapted from Judges 13–16)

"ANSWER ME SO THESE PEOPLE MAY KNOW THAT YOU ARE GOD!"

Elijah's Prayer for Fire from Heaven

Elijah was a faithful prophet of God. One day during a great drought and famine, God said to Elijah, "Go speak to the evil king Ahab, and I will send rain down on the earth." So Elijah went to Ahab.

When King Ahab saw Elijah, he said, "Is it you, the one who brings trouble to Israel?"

Elijah replied, "I have not brought trouble to Israel. But you have, because you turned away from the Lord and followed the false god Baal. So now, call together people from all over Israel to meet me at Mount Carmel. And gather together 450 men who speak for Baal."

Ahab did as Elijah said. Then Elijah came near all the people and said, "If the Lord is God, follow Him. But if Baal is god, then follow him." The people did not respond.

Then Elijah said to them, "I am the only man left who speaks for God. But here are 450 men who speak for Baal. Bring us some wood. Then you call on the name of your god, and I will call on the name of the Lord. The God who answers by creating fire is the one true God." All the people thought this battle of gods was a good idea.

So Elijah said to the men who spoke for Baal, "Call on the name of your god." They called on the name of Baal from morning until noon, saying, "O Baal, answer us." But no one answered. They jumped and danced around the altar they had made. Still, no one answered.

At noon Elijah made fun of them. He said, "Call out with a loud voice. Maybe he's

asleep." So they cried with a loud voice until evening. But no one answered. No one listened.

Then Elijah said to all the people, "Come near to me." So they did. Elijah built an altar in the name of the Lord, and he made a large ditch around it. Then he set the wood in place. He said, "Fill four jars with water and pour it on the wood." Then he said, "Do it a second time." And then, "Do it a third time." The water filled the ditch.

Elijah prayed, "O Lord, I am Your servant and have done all these things at Your word. Answer me so these people may know that You are God. Turn their hearts to You."

The fire of the Lord fell. Even though everything on and around the altar was soaking wet, the fire burned up the wood, the stones, and the dust. It even picked up the water in the ditch! All the people fell on their faces in awe. They said, "The Lord, He is God!"

Then God, who always wins over false gods, sent rain on the land.

(Adapted from 1 Kings 18)

"LORD, THERE IS NO ONE BUT YOU TO HELP IN THE BATTLE!"

Asa's Prayer for Victory

King Asa was a good king of Judah who did what was right in the eyes of the Lord. He tore down the pillars and altars that had been used to worship false gods before his reign began. He told Judah to follow the one true God and obey His laws. And the nation had peace under his rule—no one fought a war with Judah, and King Asa built strong cities during those years of peace. So he said to the people of Judah, "The land is still ours because we have followed the Lord our God. We have followed Him, and He has given us rest on every side." So they kept doing well because they followed the one true God.

But then their time of peace ended. A king named Zerah came out to fight against them. And he came out with a huge army, an army much bigger than the army of Judah.

King Asa had a lot of soldiers, brave men with shields and spears and bows and arrows. But they couldn't compare with Zerah's huge army of a million men and three hundred war wagons! Still, Asa bravely went out to meet him. Both armies made themselves ready for battle.

Asa knew there was no way the smaller and weaker army of Judah could defeat Zerah's big army without help from God. So Asa called to the Lord God and prayed, "Lord, there is no one but You to help in the battle between the powerful and the weak. So help us, please! For we trust in You. In Your name we have come against these many people. O Lord, You are our God. Do not let any army win the fight against You."

And God answered Asa's prayer. God began to destroy Judah's enemies right before the eyes of Asa and his people. The enemy ran away! Asa and the people with him went after them. Judah's enemies were destroyed. The people of Judah destroyed all the nearby cities and took every valuable thing that was in them. Then they returned to Jerusalem.

When he was in trouble, Asa prayed to God. The king knew that even though the enemy was more powerful, God could still help Judah win the battle. With God as our leader, we always walk away victorious.

(Adapted from 2 Chronicles 14)

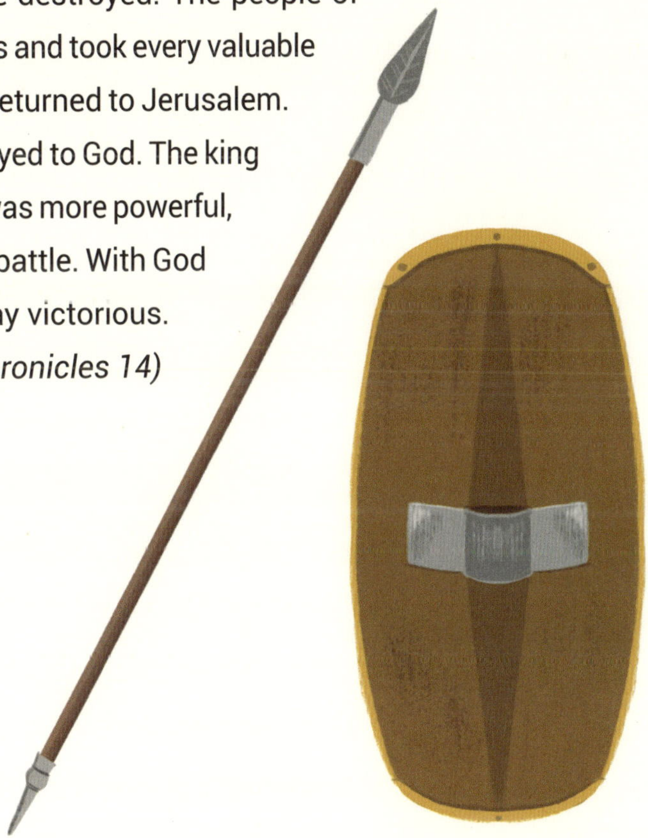

SEPTEMBER

Strength and Perseverance

When you think of strength, what does it look like to you? A superhero? A giant tree that never bends or breaks in a storm? A bodybuilder? A football player? A skyscraper built to stand in any kind of weather? A tiger or shark? The fastest swimmer? The most graceful dancer? All of these have incredible strength.

No matter how you picture strength, it's important to remember who is the mightiest of all—our almighty God. He has supernatural strength, and He is the Creator and giver of all strength. As we grow and develop our strength, we should want all of it to be based on Him. We can picture Him holding us and making us strong as we depend on Him.

Many people in the Bible learned about depending on God as their strength and depending on God as their encouragement to be persistent—to keep on going even when things were hard. We can use their stories as examples that inspire and encourage us to always let God be our source of strength. Read the following stories and see for yourself!

ONLY A SHEPHERD BOY

The Story of David

A man of Israel named David was the youngest son of Jesse. David's three oldest brothers went off to fight in battle for King Saul, who was leading the people of Israel against their enemy, the Philistines. David's job was to care for his father's sheep, until one day Jesse gave him another job—to deliver food to his brothers and check on how they were doing.

At the battlefield, the evil Philistine Goliath, a giant of a man, was teasing and taunting God's people day after day. He dared anyone to try to defeat him. This went on for forty days and forty nights, with not one man from the Israelite army willing to fight Goliath. He was too big, and they were too scared.

When David witnessed this, he was not afraid of Goliath, and he offered to fight. King Saul scoffed at the idea. But David said, "I kill lions and bears that attack my sheep. God protects me from them, and He will protect me as I fight Goliath."

So King Saul said, "Go, and God be with you." He gave his own clothes for David to wear, plus armor and a helmet to protect him.

But when David tried to strap on the king's sword and walk around, he was too uncomfortable. "I cannot wear all this," he said. "I'm not used to this kind of gear." He took it all off and prepared himself for battle with only his shepherd's staff, his sling, and five smooth stones. Then he started across the valley to confront Goliath.

Sneering, Goliath said, "Do you think I'm just a dog, since you're coming at me with only a stick?"

David replied, "You come to me with sword and spear to kill me, but I come to you in the name of the Lord Almighty, the God of Israel. You have defied Him, but today He will conquer you! Everyone here will know that the Lord rescues His people—but not with sword and spear. This is God's battle, and He will give you to us!"

David loaded his sling and launched one smooth stone at Goliath. The stone sailed through the air and struck the giant hard, right in the middle of his forehead. Goliath stumbled and fell face down. Then David ran to grab Goliath's sword, and he used it to kill the giant and cut off his head. When the Philistines saw their strongest man was dead, they all ran away, while the Israelite army shouted in victory and chased after them.

David trusted that God's great strength is mightier than giants and weapons. With God's power working in him, David was able to defeat the great Philistine giant.

(Adapted from 1 Samuel 17)

A BLAZING FIERY FURNACE

The Story of Shadrach, Meshach, and Abednego

After King Nebuchadnezzar of Babylon took over Jerusalem, he decided to have a huge gold statue built to look like a god. He ordered all the leaders in the land of Babylon to come dedicate the golden statue. As they stood before it, the king's herald announced, "When you hear the sound of the horns and harps, you must get down on your knees and worship the gold statue that King Nebuchadnezzar has set up! Anyone who does not bow down and worship will be thrown into a furnace full of hot fire."

When all the people heard the sound of the music, *almost* all of them got down and worshipped the gold statue. But three strong, smart men named Shadrach, Meshach, and Abednego refused to worship anyone but the one true God. So some men went to the king and tattled on them for not bowing down to the golden statue.

This made King Nebuchadnezzar furious, and he called for the three faithful Israelites. "Is this true?" he asked them. "I will give you one more chance to obey me, and if not, you will be thrown into the fiery furnace. Who will be able to rescue you then?"

Shadrach, Meshach, and Abednego bravely replied, "If you throw us into the fiery furnace, the God we serve is able to save us from it. But even if He does not, we will *never* serve your gods or worship the statue of gold you have set up."

The angry king ordered the furnace to be seven times hotter than normal. He commanded some of his strongest soldiers to tie up Shadrach, Meshach, and Abednego and throw them into the fire. The flames were blazing and so hot that the soldiers were killed as they threw the three friends in.

As King Nebuchadnezzar was watching all this, suddenly he leaped to his feet. "Weren't there three men we just threw in the fire?" he asked his servants.

"Of course," they replied.

"Look!" King Nebuchadnezzar said. "I see *four* men walking around in the fire, untied and unharmed, and the fourth man looks like a god!" So he called for the men to come out of the fire—and they did!

The king and all his servants and leaders gathered around them and saw that not even a hair on their heads was burned, nor any of their clothes, and there was not a scratch anywhere on them. They didn't even smell like fire!

The king could hardly believe his eyes. He said, "Praise to the God of Shadrach, Meshach, and Abednego! He sent His angel to rescue His servants who trusted in Him." And he decreed that anyone who spoke against their God would be destroyed, saying, "There is no other god who can rescue like this!"

Even under great stress and danger to their lives, Shadrach, Meshach, and Abednego persisted in their faith. They knew God had the power to save.

(Adapted from Daniel 3)

FROM DEATH TO LIFE

The Story of Lazarus

Lazarus was a good friend and follower of Jesus, and so were his sisters, Mary and Martha. When Lazarus became sick and was dying, his sisters sent word to Jesus to tell Him.

When Jesus heard this news, He said, "His sickness will not end in death. It has happened so that it will bring honor to God. And the Son of God will be honored by it too." Even though Jesus loved His friends and had heard how sick Lazarus was, He did not go to him right away. He stayed where He was with His disciples for two more days. Finally, He said to His disciples, "Let's go back to Judea. Our friend Lazarus has fallen asleep, but I am going there to wake him up."

When Jesus arrived in Bethany, He found that Lazarus had already been dead in a tomb for four days. Many Jewish people were visiting Mary and Martha to comfort them in the loss of their brother. But when Martha heard that Jesus was coming, she ran out to meet Him. She said to Jesus, "Lord, if You had been here, my brother would not have died. I know even now God will give You whatever You ask."

Jesus replied, "Your brother will rise again." And He told her, "I am the one who raises the dead and gives them life. Anyone who puts his trust in Me will live again, even if he dies. Anyone who lives and has put his trust in Me will never die. Do you believe this?"

Martha answered, "Yes, Lord, I believe that You are the Christ, the Son of God."

Then she went and called her sister Mary, and Mary got up and went to Jesus and cried at His feet.

Jesus saw her crying, and He was troubled. He said, "Where did you lay Lazarus?"

Mary and the people with her said, "Lord, come and see." Then Jesus cried too.

The Jews said, "See how much He loved Lazarus."

Jesus went to the grave with a sad heart. The grave was a hole in the side of a hill, and a stone covered the door. Jesus said, "Take the stone away." So they did. Then Jesus looked up and said, "Father, I thank You for hearing Me. I know You always hear Me. But I have said this for the people standing here, so they may believe You have sent Me." After He had said this, He called with a loud voice, "Lazarus, come out!"

Then the man who had been dead came out, still in his graveclothes with a white cloth tied around his face. Jesus said to the people, "Take off the graveclothes and let him go!"

Through God's great strength and power to heal, Lazarus who had died was once again alive!

(Adapted from John 11:1–44)

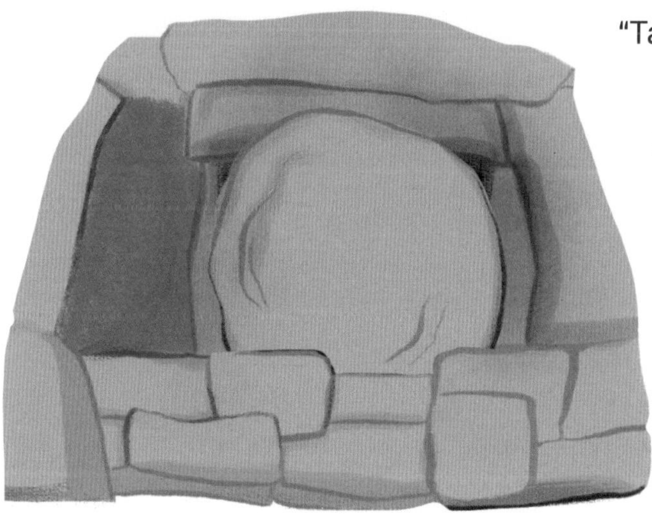

A STRONGMAN'S SECRET

The Story of Samson

The Philistines were enemies of Israel. They took all the Israelites' swords and spears so they couldn't fight. Then they robbed Israel of their crops so they would starve. The people cried to God, and God heard them.

God sent an angel to the wife of a man named Manoah. The angel told her, "You will have a son. When he grows up, he will save Israel from the Philistines. Your son must never drink any wine. His hair must never be cut. He will be a Nazirite and help Israel take away the Philistines' power." The woman named her baby Samson. When he grew up, his body was big, powerful, and strong.

One day, Samson was walking through a vineyard—a place where grapes grow. Suddenly, a huge lion appeared. It roared at Samson, ready to attack. But God's Spirit was with Samson. With all his power and strength, Samson grabbed the lion and tore it apart.

Another time, a tribe of Philistines attacked one of the tribes of Israel. The Israelites blamed Samson. They tied him up and took him to the Philistines. But Samson did something unexpected. He broke through the ropes as if they were string. He grabbed a dead mule's jawbone, and with it, he fought the Philistines until none were left.

Unfortunately, a woman who Samson loved eventually gave away the secret of his strength to the Philistines. One night while Samson slept, she let the Philistines come inside and they cut off his hair. Samson's strength was gone. The Philistines hurt him so badly that he could no longer see. Then they locked him up in their prison.

After a while, Samson's hair began to grow long again. Samson asked God to let him

use his regained strength to defeat the Philistines. God said yes. He would work out His plans through Samson. Samson stood between two tall stone pillars that held up a building where the Philistine leaders and their people were. He leaned against the pillars, pushing with all his might, and the building fell. The Philistines died, and sadly, so did Samson. But the Philistines were finally defeated.

(Adapted from Judges 13–16)

Silly Prayers

Back-to-school time can be either exciting or scary or sad—or maybe a little of all three. There are a lot of feelings when the fun of summer break ends and a new year of school begins. But we should be so thankful to God for the amazing brains He has given us. It's incredible how we can learn new things every single day. So in the times you might feel bored and blah about school, choose to thank God instead. Thank Him that He gave you such a powerful mind. Use it to learn about God and worship Him, and then ask Him to show you all the good things He designed you to know and do. The Bible tells us about some people who did not use their brains very well when they prayed—you don't want to act like them. They should have been a lot smarter in their prayers, and we can learn from their mistakes. Read the following stories and see for yourself!

"O LORD GOD, FOR SURE YOU HAVE FOOLED THESE PEOPLE!"

Jeremiah's Prayer Accusing God

Jeremiah was a prophet of God. God chose Jeremiah before he was even born. The Lord said, "Before I even formed you in your mother's womb, I knew you. Before you were born, I decided you were holy. I chose you to speak to the nations for Me."

Jeremiah replied, "God, I don't know how to speak! I am only a boy."

But God said, "Do not say, 'I am only a boy.' Go everywhere I send you, and say whatever I tell you. Don't be afraid. For I am with you to help you get out of trouble."

Then God put out His hand and touched Jeremiah's mouth and said to him, "See, I have put My words in your mouth. I have chosen you today to be over the nations and the kings, to destroy and throw down, to build and plant."

God told Jeremiah that he should not marry or have children. The Lord wanted Jeremiah to devote himself fully to speaking for God.

Jeremiah was sometimes called the weeping prophet. He was sad and cried a lot over the wicked ways of the people of Israel—because he knew God would punish them.

And though Jeremiah walked closely with God, he was not perfect. He got depressed at times. One time he prayed in a very silly way. He forgot God's goodness and truth and faithfulness, and he allowed himself to be discouraged and doubtful of God. He even began to accuse God of being dishonest with the people of Israel. He prayed, "O Lord God, for sure You have fooled these people! You told them, 'You will have peace,' when

in truth, a sword brings danger to their lives."

But God never lies. The Bible says He *cannot* lie. And so Jeremiah needed to learn a lesson from his silly prayer. He needed to trust again that God was working out His good plans, even if Jeremiah did not fully understand them. So that's what he did. No matter the sadness and pain that sometimes came from obeying God in this world, Jeremiah kept trusting God. He believed that God was teaching and loving and disciplining His people—and always providing a way for them to repent of their sin and be saved.

(Adapted from Jeremiah 1–4, 16)

"NO, I COULD NEVER DO THAT, GOD!"

Ezekiel's Prayer of Protest

Ezekiel was a prophet whose name means "strengthened by God." He preached to the people of his day about God's judgment and salvation. Sometimes God told Ezekiel to do some strange things to warn people about the danger of their sin. One day God said to Ezekiel, "Get a hard block of clay. Set it down in front of you, and draw the city of Jerusalem on it. Then build a wall around the city of clay to shut it in. You will fight a battle against it. This will be something special for the people of Israel to see."

Next God told Ezekiel to lie on his left side for 390 days. This was a sign to the nation of Israel that they would be punished for 390 years because they had turned away from God. God said, "Lie on your left side, and I will lay the people's sin on you. You will be under the weight of their sin for all the days you lie on your side."

God wanted to show people that there are consequences for sin. However, God is never happy when people are punished for their sins. He wants people to turn away from sin so He can give them the best kind of life. They can only have this kind of life through faith and obedience to Him. God said to Ezekiel, "Tell the people of Israel that I am not pleased when sinful people die. But I am pleased when they turn from their sin and live. Turn! Turn from your sinful ways, O people of Israel!"

Ezekiel must have wondered why God chose such odd ways to share His warnings and prophecies. And one day Ezekiel prayed in a silly way to God. When God told him to eat food that Ezekiel thought was unclean, the prophet said, "No, I could never do that, God!" But even as Ezekiel questioned God, the Lord loved him. And God kept using Ezekiel to speak to His beloved people of Israel.

God might work in ways that seem strange, but He is always working in ways that are best. And God's ways always lead to His perfect endings.

(Adapted from Ezekiel 2; 4; 22; 33)

"O LORD, WHY HAVE YOU HURT THESE PEOPLE?"

Moses' Prayer of Complaint to God

Before all those plagues God sent on Egypt, before the people of Israel were finally set free from their slavery, Moses had a lot of hard work to do. He had to tell the strong, scary Pharaoh that he was doing wrong! Sometimes Moses didn't think he could do what God asked. When God first called him to go to Pharaoh and lead God's people out of Egypt, Moses said, "Lord, I am not a man of words. I have never been. For I talk slowly, and it is difficult for me to speak."

So God said to him, "Who makes someone not able to speak or hear? Who makes someone blind or able to see? Is it not I, the Lord? So go now. And I will be with your mouth. I will teach you what to say."

But Moses still argued. He said, "O Lord, please, I beg you, send some other person—not me!"

This made God angry, but still he loved Moses. God even listened to Moses' silly prayer. "Aaron is your brother, and I know he can speak well," God said. "He is coming to meet you. You must speak to him and put the words in his mouth. I will be with your mouth and his mouth. I will teach you what you are to do. He will speak to the people for you. You will take this special stick in your hand and use it to make special things happen for the people to see."

But even with Aaron's help, it was no easy job to warn Pharaoh. He didn't want to let God's people go because they were slaves doing lots of free work for him. Pharaoh said, "Why should I obey your God and let Israel go? I do not know the Lord. And I will not let Israel go." Then he made the Israelites work even harder. He said, "Let more work be given to the men so they will not have time to listen to Moses' lies." Pharaoh punished the people when they couldn't do the impossible things he commanded.

The Israelites complained to Moses and Aaron, and Moses grew very discouraged. He prayed to God, "O Lord, why have You hurt these people? Why did you ever send me? Since I went to Pharaoh to speak in Your name, he has only hurt these people more. You have not set Your people free at all."

But Moses was forgetting that God works things out in His own ways, in His own perfect timing. God had not set the people free—*yet*—but He would. God always keeps His promises. And He told Moses, "Now you will see what I will do to Pharaoh. For he will be made to let them go because of My strong hand."

(Adapted from Exodus 4–6)

"GOD, I THANK YOU THAT I AM NOT LIKE OTHER MEN"

The Pharisee's Prideful Prayer

When Jesus lived on earth and taught people about God, He often used picture stories called parables. One day, His followers asked Him, "Why do You teach in picture stories?"

He answered them, "This is why I speak in picture stories. The people have eyes, but they do not see. They have ears, but they do not hear or understand. This is exactly what the prophet Isaiah said would happen." Jesus wants everyone to have eyes and ears and hearts that pay attention and understand God's truth.

One of Jesus' picture stories was about a silly way to pray and a good way to pray. He told this story to some people who were full of pride. These people did not think well of others; they mostly bragged and thought only about themselves. So Jesus said, "Two men went up to the house of God to pray. One of them was a Pharisee, a proud religious law keeper. The other was a man who collected taxes. The proud Pharisee stood and prayed like this: 'God, I thank You that I am not like other men. I am not like those who steal. I am not like those who sin. I am not even like this tax collector. I go without food two times a week so I can pray better. I always give away part of the money I earn.'"

Jesus continued, "But the tax collector stood a long way off. He would not even lift his eyes to heaven. He hit himself on his chest and said, 'God, have pity on me! I am a sinner!'" Then Jesus explained, "I tell you, this man went back to his house forgiven, and not the other man. For whoever makes himself look more important than he is will find out how little he is worth. Whoever does not try to brag about himself will be made important."

Telling God how wonderful you are, without admitting your sins and mistakes, is a silly way to pray. It is better to tell God how wonderful and good *He* is. Then be humble and honest about your own sins and mistakes. We can be grateful that God loves and forgives us no matter what.

(Adapted from Matthew 13; Luke 18)

OCTOBER

Harvest

Cool, crisp air. Pumpkins and apple cider. Hayrides and fall festivals. Raking leaves and jumping in the great big piles. Red, orange, and yellow colors painted on all the trees and floating to the ground. . . There are so many wonderful things about the season of fall! Think about your favorite fall fun activity. Then think about what a blessing it is that God gives us such a beautiful time of year, a time of harvest to bring in the good foods God helped grow. A time to remember and celebrate how God provides. Sometimes He provides exactly how we expect with exactly what we think we need. And sometimes He provides in ways we never even dreamed of. Sometimes God blesses and provides after we have done the work He guides us to do. And sometimes He provides a blessing that's just a totally sweet surprise!

So many times in God's Word, we see how God blessed and provided for His people with exactly the right thing at exactly the right time. When we learn from these people and their experiences, we can trust all the more that God is always blessing and providing for us too. Read the following stories and see for yourself!

OVERFLOWING NETS

The Story of the Fishers of Men

One day early in Jesus' ministry on earth, He was teaching on the shore of the Sea of Galilee. Many people gathered closely around Him to hear the Word of God. Then Jesus spotted two boats owned by fishermen who were done fishing for the day and were washing out their nets. Jesus decided to get in one of the boats. He asked the boat's owner, a man named Simon Peter, to paddle out into the water, just a little bit away from the shore. From there He could teach the people better because they wouldn't be so tightly crowded around Him.

When Jesus finished teaching, He said to Simon Peter, "Let's go out to deeper water. Then let down your nets to catch some fish."

But Simon said to Jesus, "Teacher, we've worked hard fishing all night, and we haven't caught even a single fish. Not one! But if You say so, we will go try again."

So they did—and they couldn't believe what happened next. They let down their nets, and suddenly those nets were nearly bursting with fish! They caught so many fish that they had to shout to ask the fishermen from the other boat to come help. Soon both boats were so full of fish that they nearly began to sink!

When Simon Peter realized what had just happened, he fell down at Jesus' feet. Simon Peter knew Jesus was extraordinary. He knew Jesus had been healing people and teaching people, and now Simon Peter was experiencing a miracle in his own life. He said to Jesus, "Please leave me, Lord. I am such a sinful man." He didn't feel worthy to be anywhere near this amazing man who could do such incredible miracles.

But Jesus said to Simon, "Do not be afraid. From now on you will fish for people."

Simon Peter wasn't totally sure what Jesus meant, but it didn't matter because he was certain that listening to Jesus was the very best choice he could make. And so, he and his partners, James and John, brought their boats back to shore and left everything to follow Jesus. They became some of Jesus' closest friends and ministry partners. And the way they fished for people was by helping Jesus as He preached the good news. If people believed that good news, it would save them from their sins; it would catch them up and bring them into the kingdom of God.

(Adapted from Luke 5:1–11)

FIVE LOAVES AND TWO FISH

The Story of the Feeding of the Five Thousand

When Jesus heard the sad news that John the Baptist had died, He wanted to be alone for a while. He went off in a boat to find a quiet place. But crowds of people wanted to hear Jesus teach, and they walked as quickly as they could from many different towns to where they had heard He was going. When Jesus got off the boat, He saw the crowds of people. He could have sent them away, since He had wanted to be alone, but He didn't. He felt full of love and kindness toward them and healed the ones who were sick.

When evening was coming, Jesus' disciples asked Him to send the crowds away. "It's getting late," they said, "and we're out here in the middle of nowhere. These people need to go into the towns and buy themselves some food."

But Jesus said, "They don't need to go away. You can give them something to eat."

The disciples were confused. Didn't Jesus see how many people were here? There were a *lot* of them—about five thousand men plus women and children too! "We have only five loaves of bread and two fish that a young boy gave us," the disciples said.

Jesus said, "Bring the loaves of bread and the fish to Me." So the disciples did. Then Jesus told the crowds of people to sit down on the grass. They sat down in big groups, some groups with fifty people and some with one hundred. Jesus took the five loaves of bread and two fish, and He looked up to heaven and gave thanks for them. Then He broke the loaves in pieces and gave them to His disciples, and the disciples gave them to the people. Jesus cut up the fish, and they shared that with everyone too. Then the five thousand men plus women and children ate and ate some more.

When they were all happily full, there was still plenty of food left over. The disciples picked up twelve baskets full of extra bread and fish after the people were finished eating. It was hard to believe all of that came from just five loaves of bread and two fish. What a miracle! Jesus had gone far above and beyond to bless the people with the food they needed.

(Adapted from Matthew 14:13–21; Mark 6:30–44; Luke 9:10–17; John 6:1–15)

REMEMBERING GOD'S WORD

The Story of the Sower and the Seeds

One day Jesus was teaching people using a story, called a parable, about a farmer who went out to plant seeds.

Jesus said that as the farmer planted the seeds, some fell by the side of the road. But the birds flew in and ate up all those seeds.

Other seeds fell between rocks. Those seeds sprouted up right away because there was hardly any soil. But then when the sun was hot and high in the sky, the seeds dried up and died because they had no roots.

Some seeds fell among thorns, but the thorns grew and did not give the seeds any room to grow.

Finally, some seeds fell on good ground and grew into a whole lot of good grain, thirty, sixty, or a hundred times more than the amount of seed planted!

Jesus explained what He meant with this parable. He said the seed that fell beside the road is like those who hear the message about God's kingdom but don't understand it. Then, like the birds, the evil one comes and steals the seed of faith that was planted in their hearts.

The seed on the rocky soil is like those who hear the message and instantly believe it with joy. But since their faith doesn't have deep roots, it doesn't last long. They fall away from faith as soon as they have problems or are hurt or teased for believing God's Word.

The seed that fell among thorns is like those who hear God's word but quickly crowd out the message with the worries of this life and wanting to have lots of money, so nothing good grows.

The seed that fell on good soil is like those who truly hear and understand God's Word and produce a harvest of thirty, sixty, or even a hundred times more than the amount of seed planted!

With every parable Jesus taught, He shared truth to help people have growing faith in Him as the Son of God—and provide everlasting life.

(Adapted from Matthew 13:3–23; Mark 4:2–20; Luke 8:4–15)

THE SCARLET ROPE

The Story of Rahab

After Moses died, Joshua became the next leader of the Israelite people. He sent two men into the land of Canaan and told them, "Go and spy out the land, especially Jericho."

So they went into Jericho and came to the house of a woman named Rahab. But someone found out and told the king of Jericho about the spies. The king sent a message to Rahab that said, "Bring out the men who have gone into your house. They came to spy on our land."

But Rahab had taken the two spies and hidden them. She said, "Yes, the men came to me, but I didn't know where they were from and I don't know where they went. If you go after them quickly, you will catch them." In reality she had brought the spies up to the roof of her house and had hidden them under the grain she stored there. The king's men went after them on the road to the Jordan River.

Before the spies went to sleep for the night, Rahab went up to them on her roof. "I know that the Lord has given you the land," she said. "The Lord your God is God in heaven above and on earth below. I've been kind to you, so I beg you to promise me that you will show kindness to my family. When you take the land, do not kill my father and mother and my brothers and sisters and all who belong to them. Please save us from death."

The spies promised to be faithful to her as long as she did not tell anyone about their plans. Then Rahab let them down by a rope through the window and told them to hide for three days in the hill country before returning to their people.

The spies said to her, "Tie this red rope in the window you let us down through. Bring your father and mother, your brothers, and all those of your father's house into your home. If anyone goes out into the street, it will be his own fault if he is killed. But if anyone who is with you in the house is hurt, we will take the blame. But you must not betray us."

She agreed. Then she sent them away and tied the red rope in the window.

The Israelite spies had needed help, and God provided Rahab at exactly the right time. And when Joshua and the Israelites took over Jericho and entered the land of Canaan as God had promised, Rahab and her family's lives were saved. They reaped a great reward because Rahab had trusted God and helped the Jewish spies.

(Adapted from Joshua 2, 6)

Prayers for Wisdom

The harvest season is a time to be thankful for the good things that were grown all summer long—apples and pumpkins and other yummy fruits and vegetables. Does your mouth water when you think of your favorite fall foods? We can be grateful for the farmers who help us have such wonderful treats! If those farmers don't work hard at sowing (which means planting seeds) and then tending the crops with care, they will never get to celebrate the reaping, which is all about gathering up the goodness. While farmers sow seeds to grow plants, we can sow in prayer. We sow in prayer by talking with God and taking good care of our relationship with Him. We ask Him for what we need, and we ask Him to protect and bless and teach and guide us. When we pray like that, we reap wisdom and closeness with our heavenly Father. That sure is a gathering of goodness! The Bible tells us about people who sowed in prayer and reaped in wisdom from God, and we can learn from their examples. Read the following stories and see for yourself!

"LORD, YOU KNOW THE HEARTS OF ALL MEN"

The Disciples' Prayer for Wisdom in Replacing Judas

After Jesus had suffered and died on the cross, He rose again! After His resurrection, He proved Himself alive by showing Himself to many people for forty days and teaching about the kingdom of God.

One day with His disciples, Jesus said, "You will receive power when the Holy Spirit comes into your lives. You will tell about Me in the city of Jerusalem and over all the countries and to the ends of the earth." Then, while they were looking at Him, He was taken up to heaven! A cloud carried Him away so they could not see Him. They were still looking up to heaven, watching Him go, when two men dressed in white suddenly stood beside them. They said, "Why are you still standing here looking up to heaven? Jesus will return in the same way you saw Him go up."

So Jesus' followers decided to go back to Jerusalem. When they came into the city, they went up to a room on the second floor where they stayed and prayed together. Women who followed Jesus—including Mary, His mother—were there, along with Jesus' brothers.

Not long after, Peter realized it was time to replace the disciple Judas, who had turned against Jesus. He got up in front of about 120 followers of Jesus and said, "It happened as the Scriptures said it would. They told about Judas, who would betray Jesus and hand Him over to be killed. Judas was one of our group and had a part in our work. But he is gone now." Peter went on, "The man to take the place of Judas should be one

of these men who walked along with us when the Lord Jesus was on earth. He must have been with us from the day Jesus was baptized by John to the day Jesus was taken up to heaven, so he can tell others that he saw Jesus raised from the dead."

So they brought two men in front of the big group of followers. Their names were Joseph and Matthias. Then the followers prayed together, "Lord, You know the hearts of all men. Show us which of these two men You have chosen to take the place of Judas and be a missionary." Then they drew names, and the name of Matthias was chosen. He was added to the group of disciples.

God knows the hearts of all people. Like Jesus' followers back in Bible times, let's pray together with other believers for His wisdom, His leading, and His will to be done.

(Adapted from Acts 1)

"GIVE ME AN UNDERSTANDING HEART"

Solomon's Prayer for Wisdom

King David of Israel had said to his son Solomon, "Be strong and do what the Lord your God tells you. Walk in His ways. Keep His laws and His Word. Then you will succeed in all that you do and in every place you go." And when David died, Solomon became the new king of Israel.

King Solomon wanted to do as his father, David, had said. He wanted to follow God's ways and keep God's laws, so God wanted to bless Solomon. One night God came to Solomon in a special dream and said, "Ask what you wish Me to give you."

Solomon could have asked God for anything at all, but he said, "God, You have made me king in place of my father, David. But I am only a little child. I do not know how to start or finish. I am among so many of Your people—too many to count! So please give me an understanding heart to judge Your people and know the difference between good and bad."

Solomon had made a very good request! He knew that wisdom from God was far more valuable than any treasure.

Because Solomon had chosen so well, God wanted to bless him even more. He said to Solomon, "You have asked for this and not for a long life for yourself. You have not asked for riches. But you have asked for understanding to know what is right. Because you have asked this, I have done what you said. See, I have given you a wise and understanding heart. No one has been like you before, and no one will ever be like you. And I also give

you what you have not asked. I give you both riches and honor. And if you walk in My ways and keep My laws and Word as your father did, I will allow you to live a long time."

When we choose to ask God for wisdom rather than riches, we also please Him, just like Solomon did. God is our good, heavenly Father who loves to bless us for choosing what's best.

When Solomon woke up from his dream, he returned to Jerusalem. He praised and worshipped God and hosted a great feast for all his servants. King Solomon did not rule Israel perfectly, but he did many good things. For many years he listened to and learned from God, using the understanding he had asked for. And the people he ruled were amazed because they could see his wisdom from God.

(Adapted from 1 Kings 2–3)

"SHOW ME SOMETHING TO PROVE THAT IT IS YOU WHO SPEAKS WITH ME"

Gideon's Prayer for God's Assurance and Direction

When God's people were under the control of the cruel Midianites, they became very poor and weak. So they cried out to God for help. God sent a prophet to remind the people of Israel that even though He had done so much for them in the past, they had disobeyed Him and worshipped fake gods.

Then the angel of the Lord went to an Israelite named Gideon. The man was working to hide his food from the Midianites.

The angel said, "The Lord is with you! You are a mighty hero, a powerful soldier!"

Gideon replied, "Then why has all this happened to us? The Lord has left us alone and put us under the power of the Midianites."

And the angel, who was really God, said, "You are strong, and you can rescue Israel from the Midianites. I am sending you."

Gideon said to Him, "O Lord, how can I save Israel? My family is the weakest around here. And I am the youngest in my father's house."

But God said to him, "For sure I will be with you. You will destroy Midian."

Gideon still wasn't sure. So he asked God, "If I have found favor in Your eyes, please show me something to prove that it is You who speaks with me. I ask of You, do not leave here until I return to You with my gift and lay it before You."

And God said, "I will stay until you return."

Then Gideon went into his house. He prepared some meat and made bread. He put the meat in a basket and the water from boiling the meat in a pot. Then he brought all these things out and set them down in front of a tree.

The angel of God said to him, "Take the meat and the bread and lay them on this rock. Then pour out the water." And Gideon did. Then the angel of the Lord sent fire to burn up the meat and the bread, and the angel disappeared. So Gideon knew that he had seen the angel of the Lord. And he said, "I am afraid, O Lord God! For now I have seen the angel of the Lord face-to-face."

But God said to Gideon, "Peace be with you. Do not be afraid. You will not die."

Then Gideon built an altar there to the Lord. He gave it the name The Lord Is Peace.

It took some time for Gideon to really trust God. But by talking with God and asking for faith, Gideon was able to do amazing things. We can do the same! Talk to God when you're confused or afraid. He'll be happy to give you the wisdom and courage you need.

(Adapted from Judges 6)

"MAY THE LORD CHOOSE SOMEONE WHO WILL LEAD THEM"

Moses' Prayer for a New Leader of Israel

Moses was an extraspecial leader and prophet of God. The Lord met him face-to-face. There was no one like him to speak for God in Israel and do such powerful works from God in Egypt. Yet after all Moses did, after leading the Israelites round and round in the wilderness, he was not allowed to enter the land God had promised. How sad!

But why? Because God once told Moses to speak to a rock so that it would pour out much-needed water for the people of Israel. They had been suffering with no water and were very thirsty. But Moses decided to do things his own way rather than God's way. Moses hit the rock with his walking stick! And there were consequences for that big mistake. God said to Moses, "Because you were not faithful to Me that time and you did not honor Me as holy among the people of Israel, you will not go into the land I am giving the people of Israel. You will only see it from far away."

Moses was disappointed, but he still remained faithful to God. When it was nearly time for the people to enter the Promised Land, Moses knew the people would need a new leader to go with them since he couldn't. He prayed, "May the Lord choose someone who will lead them. Someone to come before this community. That way, the Lord's people will not be like sheep without a shepherd."

Moses could have been bitter and angry because of God's decision not to allow him to enter the Promised Land. But he wasn't. He loved and honored God. He had wisdom and humility, and he loved the people of Israel and wanted them to have a caring leader. That man turned out to be Joshua.

After Moses prayed, God said, "Take Joshua, son of Nun, a man who has a spirit of leadership, and lay your hand on him. Have him stand before the priest and everyone else, and commission him in their presence. Give him some of your authority so the whole Israelite community will listen to him. Then he and all the Israelites will go out, and at his command, they will come into the land."

Moses obeyed. He took Joshua and laid his hands on him to make him the new leader. Maybe someday *you'll* be a leader among God's people. Right now, learn His Word and obey what it says. That's the best way to prepare for His service.

(Adapted from Numbers 20; 27; Deuteronomy 34)

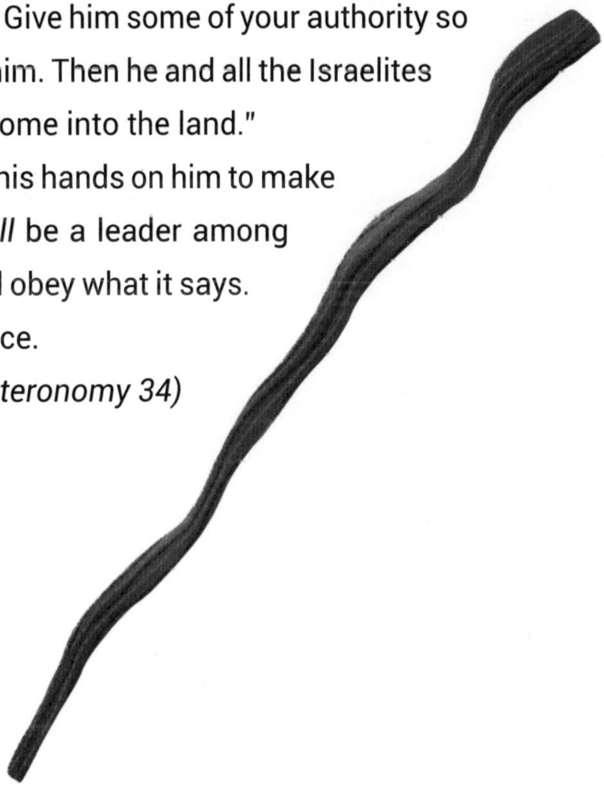

NOVEMBER

Thanksgiving

In everything, give thanks, the Bible says (1 Thessalonians 5:18). It's easy to read that scripture and think of good things to be thankful for—family, friends, your home, your favorite toys, clothes to wear and good food to eat, fun family vacations, and on and on. But sometimes hard things are happening, and you might wonder, *Really, in* everything *I should give thanks? Even when I'm sick with a fever? Even when I've lost my favorite toy? Even when my friends are being mean? Even when I have lots of homework? Even when I get in trouble with my parents?*

Yes, in all those things, give thanks. You don't have to be grateful for the hard thing itself, but you should be grateful that God never leaves you alone and will help you through any hard thing. Plus He will teach you valuable lessons during difficult times. And you can be grateful for the fact that hard situations give you a chance to grow closer to Him as you depend on Him more. The month of November is a time of great thanksgiving, celebrated by feasting together with family and friends. You can also take time to read about people of the Bible who had much to be thankful for. Read the following stories and see for yourself!

ALL SHE HAD

The Story of the Widow Who Gave Two Mites

One day after Jesus had been teaching in the temple courts, He sat down near the collection boxes for the temple treasury. That was where people put money for offerings to God. Jesus watched as many rich people gave large amounts of money. This wasn't hard for them to do because they were so rich that they had plenty of money to share. But then Jesus watched one woman, who was terribly poor and had no husband, drop in two very small copper coins. Added together, the two coins weren't even worth one whole cent.

Jesus saw this, and He called out to His disciples, "This is the truth—this poor widow has given more money than all the others."

How could this be? The widow had only given two small coins that didn't even amount to a penny! And the rich people had given a whole bunch of money—a whole lot more than the poor widow.

But Jesus said, "The rich people put in money they didn't even need because they have so much extra. But the poor widow has nothing extra. She needed every bit of her money to live on, but still she gave it all to God."

The poor widow understood true gratitude and giving. Even though she had practically nothing, she was thankful for what she did have—so thankful that she wanted to give it all back to God. She trusted God to provide for her no matter what, and she had great big faith that inspired her to give in a great big way.

(Adapted from Mark 12:41–44; Luke 21:1–4)

LIVING WATER

The Story of the Woman at the Well

One day on His travels, Jesus came near a town in Samaria called Sychar. It was about noon, and He was tired, so He sat down near a well. His disciples had gone into the town to get food. When a Samaritan woman came to get water from the well, Jesus asked her, "Could you please give Me a drink?"

Usually Jewish people had nothing to do with Samaritan people. So the woman asked Jesus, "Why are You asking me for a drink?"

But it didn't matter to Jesus that the woman was Samaritan. He loved every person, no matter what country they were from. He said to her, "If you only knew how wonderful the gift is that God wants to give to you, you would actually be the one asking *Me* for water. And then I would give you living water."

The woman didn't understand. She said to Jesus, "Where will You get this water? This well is deep, and You don't have any kind of jug with You for fetching water."

Jesus said to her, "Whoever drinks the water from this well will be thirsty again. But whoever drinks the water that I give will never be thirsty. The water that I give to people becomes a well of life inside that lasts forever."

The woman said, "Sir, please give me this water so I will never be thirsty."

Then Jesus spoke more with the woman, and she realized He knew everything about her—even though she had never told Him. She began to understand that He must truly be Jesus Christ, the Son of God. She was amazed, and she left her water jug at the well and went back to town to tell the people there, "Come with me and see a man who told me everything I ever did!"

Many Samaritans believed in Jesus because of what she told them about Him. And they went to Jesus and listened to Him. Then they invited Him to stay in their town. As more people listened to Jesus' teaching, many more believed in Him. They said to the woman at the well, "Now we believe not just because of what you said about Jesus but because we have heard Him ourselves too. We know for sure that this man really is the Savior of the world who saves people from the punishment of their sins."

(Adapted from John 4:4–42)

GOD MAKES A PROMISE

The Story of Abraham and Sarah

When a man named Abram was ninety-nine years old, God came to him and said, "I am Almighty God. If you obey Me and are faithful to Me, I will keep a covenant, a forever promise, with you that you will have a huge family and be the father of many nations."

Abram fell on his face at this news! He didn't have any children at all, so how could this be?

Still, God said to him, "You will be the father of many nations, and from now on your name will be not Abram but Abraham. Many people will come from you in your family, even kings! I will make My covenant with you and your children after you through their whole lives forever. I will give to you and your children after you all the land of Canaan forever, and I will always be your God."

About his wife, God said to Abraham, "Do not call her Sarai, because Sarah will be her name now. I will bless her and you with a baby son. She will be the mother of many nations."

Abraham fell on his face again and laughed. He said to himself, "How can I have a son now? I am too old! And how can Sarah have a baby? She is ninety years old."

But God promised Abraham, "Your wife Sarah will give birth to your son. And you must give him the name Isaac. I will make a covenant with him and all of his family after him."

Later on, God appeared to Abraham again and said, "I will come back to you about this time next year, and your wife will have a son."

Sarah overheard this, and she laughed.

And God knew she laughed and said to Abraham, "Why did she laugh? Is anything too hard for the Lord?"

Sarah was afraid and so she lied and said, "I did not laugh."

But God knew the truth and told her, "Yes, you did laugh." Still, He blessed Sarah and Abraham, just as He had promised. When their son was born, they named him Isaac, which means "laughter." Sarah said, "God has brought me laughter, and anyone who hears about how we had our son at such old ages will laugh too."

God had kept His promise, and Abraham and Sarah knew He would continue to keep His promises, and they were full of thanks.

(Adapted from Genesis 17–18; 21)

LOST AND FOUND!

The Story of the Prodigal Son

Jesus told stories called parables to help teach good lessons. One of His parables was about a man who had two sons. The younger of the two sons said to his father, "Let me have my inheritance, the part of the family riches that will be given to me."

So the father divided all that he owned between his two sons. The younger son took all his inheritance and went to another country far away. He didn't work or use his money wisely. He spent everything on living a wild and foolish life. After all his money was gone, he was hungry, but there had been a famine so there was no food in the land. The only job he could find was to feed pigs, and he was so hungry he was ready to eat the same food the pigs ate. Then he began to think about what he had done. He said to himself, "My father pays many men who work for him, and they have everything they need plus extra. And here I am nearly starving to death. I should go home to my father. I will say to him, 'Father, I have sinned against heaven and against you. I am not good enough to be called your son. But could I work for you?'"

So the son got up and went to his father. And while he was still a long way off, his father saw him and felt full of love and kindness toward him. He ran to his son and threw his arms around him and kissed him. The son said, “Father, I have sinned against heaven and against you. I am not good enough to be called your son."

But the father said to his workmen, “Hurry! Get the best coat and put it on him. Put a ring on his hand and shoes on his feet. Bring the fat calf and kill it so we can eat it. Let's be glad because my son was lost and now he is found. Let's eat and have a good time."

As the older son was coming near the house, he heard the music and dancing of the welcome home party for his younger brother. When he realized what was going on, he would not go inside. He was jealous and angry that his father was treating the runaway brother so well.

But the father said to him, “My son, you are with me all the time. All that I have is yours. It is right and good that we should have a party and be happy. We have so much to be thankful for. Your brother was lost and now he is found."

(Adapted from Luke 15:11–32)

Helpless Prayers

Thanksgiving is a time to be grateful for all the good things in your life—your family and your friends, your pets and your home, your toys and all the fun things you get to do. And don't forget the good food you get to eat! You can be thankful for the not-so-good things too, for the way they help you depend on God's love and care to get you through. Hard times in our lives make us cry out to God in what might feel like hopeless prayers. We feel helpless and can't think of any good answer for the problems we face. But then when we see God answer our prayers in amazing, miraculous ways, we are filled with gratitude like never before! Have you ever been through something like that? The Bible tells us about people who have been, and we can learn from them. Read the following stories and see for yourself!

"YOU HAVE BROUGHT ME UP FROM THE PIT, GOD!"

Jonah's Prayer from Inside the Big Fish

Jonah was a man who found himself in the belly of a big fish! How did that happen? Well, the problem started when God said to him, "Go to the city of Nineveh. The people there are very wicked. Tell them I have seen their terrible sins, and I am sending My judgment." But Jonah didn't want to go to Nineveh. He'd heard about how bad it was there, and he wanted nothing to do with that city or its people. So Jonah tried to run away from God. He got on a boat and set sail for another land.

But God is everywhere, and no matter how he tried, Jonah couldn't run away or hide from Him. God caused a strong wind and a big storm on the sea where Jonah was sailing. The storm was so dangerous that Jonah's boat was about to break up and sink. All the sailors were scared, and they decided that the storm was Jonah's fault. "You'd better throw me into the sea," he said. "Then the seas will calm down. I know this bad storm has happened because of me."

So the sailors prayed to God for mercy and then threw Jonah into the sea. Suddenly, the storm stopped, just like Jonah said it would. Then the sailors worshipped the one true God and promised to serve Him.

God still had plans for Jonah! He sent a big fish to swallow Jonah, but it didn't hurt him. Jonah simply sat in the slimy, stinky stomach of that fish for three days and three nights. While he sat, he prayed. "God, You threw me into the deep waters, to the bottom of the sea. The sea was all around me. Weeds were around my head. I sank down. But You have brought me up from the pit, God! While I was losing all my strength, I remembered You. And my prayer came to You. I will give You what I have promised because You are the one who saves."

Jonah didn't just pray when he felt helpless. He also honored and worshipped God—even from the stomach of a big fish! So we know that no matter how strange or hard or sad something is, we can worship and feel grateful too. And God listens and answers and blesses us when we do.

(Adapted from Jonah 1–2)

"WE ONLY HAVE FIVE LOAVES OF BREAD AND TWO FISH!"

The Disciples' Prayer for Jesus to Help Feed the People

Everywhere Jesus went when He lived on earth, crowds of people wanted to hear Him teach. They came from many different towns as quickly as they could to wherever they learned He was going. One day after Jesus had taken some quiet time, He got off a boat to discover even more people wanting His teaching and His healing. He felt sorry for them. But it was getting later, and evening was coming. So Jesus' disciples asked Him to send the crowds away. The people needed to eat, but they were in the middle of nowhere.

Jesus told the disciples, "You can give them something to eat."

What? They didn't have a market nearby or a kitchen to use. Didn't Jesus see how many people there were? There were a *lot* of them—about five thousand men plus women and children too! "We only have five loaves of bread and two fish, which a young boy gave us," they said to Jesus. They didn't know how to feed so many people with such a small amount of food! They felt totally helpless.

So Jesus said to the disciples, "Bring the loaves of bread and the fish to Me." And they did. Then Jesus told the crowds of people to sit down on the grass. They sat down in big groups. Jesus took the five loaves of bread and two fish, and He looked up to heaven and gave thanks for them. Then He broke the loaves in pieces and gave them to His disciples, and the disciples gave them to the people. Jesus cut up the fish, and they shared that with everyone too. Then the men, women, and children ate until ther bellies were full.

When everyone was done eating, there was still plenty of food left over. The disciples picked up twelve baskets full of extra bread and fish—one basket for each disciple. It was hard to believe all that came from just five loaves of bread and two fish. What a miracle! Jesus had gone far above and beyond to bless the people with the food they needed. Though the disciples had felt helpless, they learned that when Jesus asks us to do something, even if it seems totally impossible, we can pray to Him. Then He will provide exactly what we need, exactly when we need it!

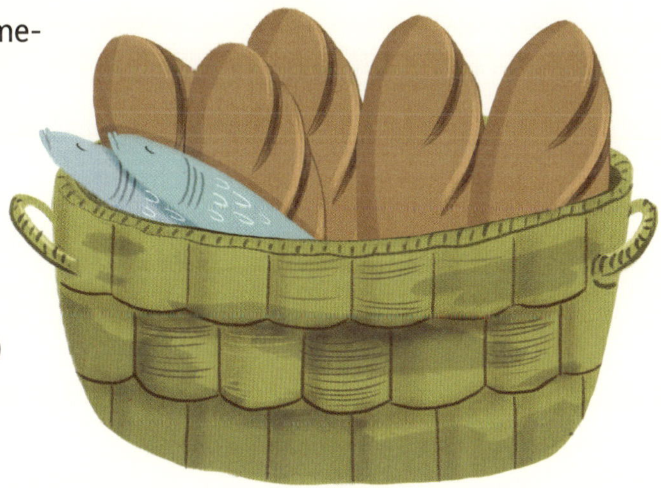

(Adapted from Matthew 14; Mark 6; Luke 9; John 6)

"THE BURDEN IS TOO MUCH"

Moses' Prayer for Relief

One day when God's people were still wandering in the wilderness, they began to complain about the food that God provided. They had a miracle bread called manna that fell from the sky each night, but they wanted something else. The people whined and cried out, "If only we had meat to eat! We remember the fish we ate in Egypt—also the cucumbers, melons, leeks, onions, and garlic. But now we don't even want to eat because we never see anything but this manna!"

The manna was plain and tasted like something made with olive oil. But it was what God had provided.

God became angry at all the complaining, and Moses was troubled. He questioned the Lord, saying, "Why have You brought this trouble on me, Your servant? What have I done to displease You that You put the burden of all these people on me? Why did You tell me to lead them to the land You promised to their ancestors? Where can I get meat for all these people? They keep wailing to me, 'Give us meat to eat!' I cannot carry all these people by myself! The burden is too much, too heavy for me."

God listened to Moses' cries and said, "Bring Me seventy of Israel's elders who are known as leaders among the people. Have them come to the tent of meeting, that they may stand there with you. I will come down and speak with you there, and I will take some of the power of the Spirit that is on you and put it on them. They will share the burden of the people with you so that you will not have to carry it alone."

God also promised to send meat to the people. "How is that possible?" Moses asked.

The Lord answered, "Is My power limited? Now you will see whether or not what I say will come true for you." God soon sent birds called quail. There were so many that they surrounded the Israelites' camp, and the people gathered up many of them to eat. There was plenty of meat now! But some of the people got sick because of their complaints and ungratefulness.

Moses learned that when he couldn't do a big job, God would listen to his prayers and provide help.

(Adapted from Numbers 11)

"MY GOD, WHY HAVE YOU LEFT ME ALONE?"

Jesus' Prayer on the Cross

When Jesus was about to be crucified, the soldiers and the people who hated Him treated Him terribly. They took off His clothes and put a scarlet coat on Him. They put a crown of thorns on His head. They put a stick in His right hand and got on their knees before Him to make fun of Him. They mocked Him as they said, "Hello, King of the Jews!" They spit on Him. They hit Him on the head. And after they had made fun of Him, they led Him away to be nailed to a cross.

On the cross, over His head, they put a sign that said THIS IS JESUS, THE KING OF THE JEWS.

Two robbers were nailed to crosses beside Jesus. One was on His right side, and one was on His left. Those who walked by shook their heads and laughed at Him. They said, "Save Yourself. If You are the Son of God, come down from the cross."

The head religious leaders and the teachers of the Law and the other leaders made fun of Him too. They said, "He saved others, but He cannot save Himself. If He is the King of the Jews, let Him come down from the cross. Then we will believe in Him. Let God save Him now if God cares for Him. Jesus said He was the Son of God."

From noon until three o'clock on that day, it was dark over all the land. At about three o'clock Jesus cried with a loud voice, "My God, My God, why have You left Me alone?" Jesus gave another loud cry and then gave up His spirit and died.

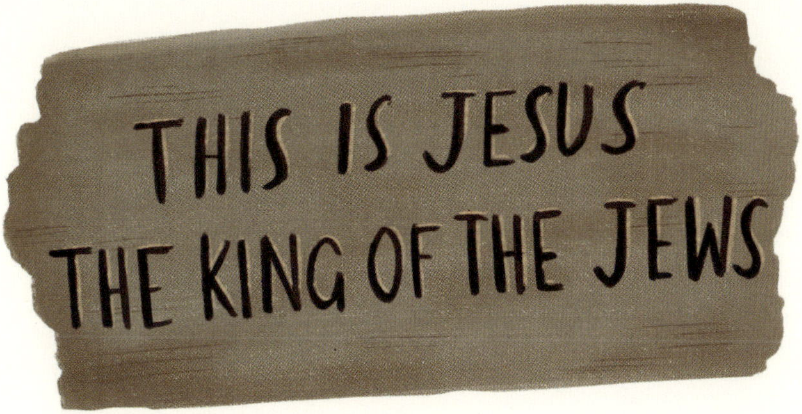

Jesus must have felt helpless and alone as He took all the sins of every person, suffering and dying in their place. But God's plans were being accomplished. He was working in a powerful way to provide salvation and eternal life for all who trust in Jesus.

Immediately at Jesus' death, the curtain in the house of God was torn in two from top to bottom. The earth shook, and big rocks split in two. Graves were opened, and the bodies of many of God's people who were dead were raised to life! The captain of the soldiers and those with him who were watching Jesus saw all the things that were happening. They saw the earth shake, and they were terrified. They said, "For sure, this Man really was the Son of God."

And this Man is the one who saves you from sin when you believe in Him. Have you asked Jesus to forgive your sins and change your life?

(Adapted from Matthew 27)

DECEMBER

Christmas

At the end of every year comes the biggest celebration of all—one great big birthday party for Jesus! That's what the Christmas season is all about. Jesus is born! We celebrate the gift that He was and still is to the world. Jesus came once as a baby and lived and loved others so well. Then He died as punishment for the sins of all people but rose to life again to defeat death and offer life forever to those who believe in Him. He was the hope people were waiting on, and He is still that hope for everyone today. At Christmastime we celebrate that God became a human being in Jesus. Christmas shows how much God loves us and wants to be close to us.

How do you celebrate Jesus at Christmastime? Do you give and get gifts to remember how God gave us the most incredible gift of Jesus? Do you eat birthday cake in honor of His special day? Do you share love and serve others? Do you decorate a tree and sing carols and bake cookies? All of these and so much more are wonderful ways to enjoy the Christmas season!

The most important way to celebrate in December is to keep Jesus in mind in all you think and say and do. God's Word gives us many details about the miraculous events surrounding Jesus' birth that help us to remember to honor and love Him during this special season. Read the following stories and see for yourself!

A HEAVENLY GREETING

The Story of Mary, Mother of Jesus

To the village of Nazareth in Galilee, God sent the angel Gabriel to a young unmarried girl named Mary. She was engaged to a man named Joseph, who was a descendant of King David. Gabriel appeared to Mary and said, "Greetings! You are highly favored among all women. The Lord is with you!"

Mary was troubled and confused by the angel and his greeting. What could this mean?

The angel said, "Don't be afraid, Mary. You are blessed by God, and you are going to give birth to a son, and you are to name Him Jesus. He will be great and called the Son of the Most High. He will reign over all of Israel, and His kingdom will never end."

"But how is this possible?" Mary asked. "I'm not married, and I am a virgin."

"This will happen by the power of the Holy Spirit," the angel said. "The baby you have will be holy and will be the Son of God. Your cousin Elizabeth is going to have a baby too, even though she is old and has never been able to have children before. Nothing is impossible with God!"

And Mary said, "I am willing to serve God however He asks. May everything you have just said come true."

Right away, Mary got ready and hurried to her cousin Elizabeth's house in a little town in the hill country of Judea where Elizabeth lived with her husband, Zechariah. As soon as Elizabeth saw Mary and heard her greeting, Elizabeth felt the baby growing inside her leap for joy. She was excited and filled with the Holy Spirit. She happily told Mary, "You are blessed among women, and blessed is the child you are carrying. Blessed are the women who believe that what the Lord has said will happen!"

And Mary sang a special song of praise, like this: "My heart sings with thanks for my Lord. And my spirit is happy in God my Savior. I was just an unimportant servant girl, but the Lord has blessed me, and from now on all people will honor me. God has done great things for me. His name is holy. The loving-kindness of the Lord is given to the people of all times who honor Him."

Though she was shocked and confused at first by the angel Gabriel's greeting, Mary happily agreed to the good plans God had to bless her with a son—an extraordinary son who would be the greatest blessing to all people forevermore.

(Adapted from Luke 1:26–55)

ANOTHER MIRACULOUS BIRTH

The Story of John the Baptist

The angel Gabriel had told Mary, "Your cousin Elizabeth is going to have a baby too, even though she is old and has never been able to have children before. Nothing is impossible with God!" And Gabriel was exactly right. Soon after Mary left Elizabeth's home, it was time for Elizabeth to have her baby. She gave birth to a son, and Elizabeth and Zechariah knew exactly what to name him. The angel Gabriel had appeared to Zechariah and foretold the baby's birth and said he would be a very special baby with a very special purpose—and his name must be John.

Zechariah was filled with the Holy Spirit and said to his new son, "You will be called a prophet of God, the Most High. You will go on before the Lord to prepare the way for Him, to tell people about salvation through forgiveness of sin."

Young John grew up and became strong and went to live in the wilderness until it was time for him to prepare the way for Jesus. He wore a coat made of camel's hair and a belt of leather. His favorite foods were grasshoppers and wild honey. Then one day God called him out of the wilderness to start baptizing many people. Baptism was a washing with water for people to show that they were sorry for their sin and wanted to turn away from it and be saved. This is why John was called John the Baptist. Many people thought John was the promised Messiah, but John assured them that he was just helping prepare the way for when Jesus, the true Messiah, would begin traveling and teaching. He said to the people, "I baptize you with water, but there is one coming who is greater. I am not good enough to even help Him take off His shoes. He will baptize you with the Holy Spirit."

And then one day Jesus came from Galilee to the Jordan River to be baptized by John. "I need to be baptized by *You*," John said to Jesus. "But You're coming to *me*?"

And Jesus said, "Yes, let this be done now. It is right for Me to be baptized by you."

And John agreed, and he baptized Jesus. When Jesus went up out of the water of the Jordan River, heaven opened up and the Spirit of God came down like a dove and rested on Jesus. And a voice from heaven said, "This is My Son. I love Him and am very happy with Him."

John's miraculous birth was important to the story of Jesus' miraculous birth. God had incredible plans for the lives of these special cousins who were born just months apart.

(Adapted from Matthew 3;
Mark 1:1–11; Luke 1;
John 1:1–34)

BIRTH OF A KING

The Story of Baby Jesus

When the Roman emperor Caesar Augustus ordered that every person must travel to their hometown to take part in a census, Joseph and Mary traveled to Bethlehem to register. Bethlehem was known as the city of David, and Joseph went there because he was from the family of David. While Joseph and Mary were in Bethlehem, the time came for the baby Jesus to be born. But so many people were in town to register that there was no place for them to stay. All the rooms at the inn were full. So in a stable for animals, Mary gave birth to baby Jesus and wrapped Him in cloth and put Him in the manger for His bed.

Out in the fields nearby, shepherds were watching over their sheep at night. Then an angel of the Lord came to them, shining brightly with God's glory, and the shepherds were afraid. But the angel said, "Don't be afraid. I have good and joyful news for all people. Today, the Savior has been born in the city of David. He is Christ the Lord. This is how you will know it's Him. You will find the baby wrapped in cloth lying in a manger where cattle are fed."

Suddenly many angels at once appeared, praising and thanking God. They said, "Glory to God in the highest, and peace to everyone on earth who pleases Him."

The angels went back to heaven, and the shepherds decided to go right to Bethlehem to see what the angel of the Lord had just told them about. They hurried and found Mary and Joseph and the baby Jesus too—and He was lying in a manger. When they saw Jesus, they told everyone they could about what the angel said about Him. All who heard it were amazed. But Mary hid all these words in her heart and treasured them. The shepherds

went back to the fields, full of joy. They thanked God for all they had heard and seen.

When the baby was eight days old, He was officially named Jesus at the temple. A few weeks later, Mary and Joseph took baby Jesus to Jerusalem to present Him to God. In Jerusalem, a man named Simeon eagerly waited for the Messiah to come and rescue Israel. The Holy Spirit was with him and had made it known to him that he would not die until he had seen the Messiah. When he was in the temple where Mary and Joseph had Jesus with them, Simeon took Jesus in his arms, praised God, and said, "Lord, now let me die in peace, as You have said. My eyes have seen the one who will save people from the punishment of their sins."

(Adapted from Luke 2:1–35)

THE RISING STAR

The Story of the Wise Men

Jesus was born in Bethlehem in the country of Judea during the time when Herod was king. Soon after Jesus' birth, some wise men came to Jerusalem from the East. They asked, "Where is the King of the Jews who has been born? We saw His star in the East, and we came to worship Him."

King Herod heard this and was jealous and worried about who this new king might be. He called together all the religious leaders and teachers of the Jews to ask them where Christ was to be born. They said to him, "In Bethlehem of Judea."

Herod met with the wise men secretly and sent them on to Bethlehem, saying, "Go and find the child, and let me know when you do so that I can go and worship Him too."

So the wise men went on their way, led by the star they had seen in the East. It stopped over the place where Jesus was, and they were filled with joy. When they found Jesus with His mother, Mary, they bowed down and worshipped Him. They gave Him gifts of gold and frankincense and myrrh. When it was time to leave, they went back to their country a different way than they had come. They wanted to stay far away from King Herod because God warned them in a dream that the king wanted to harm Jesus.

After the wise men left, an angel of the Lord came to Joseph in a dream. He said, "Get up and take Jesus and His mother to Egypt. Go as fast as you can and stay there until you hear from me. Herod is going to look for Jesus to kill Him." So, during the night Joseph got up and left with Jesus and Mary for Egypt. This happened to fulfill what God had said long before through an early prophet: "I called My Son out of Egypt."

When Herod learned that the wise men had tricked him, he was very angry. He sent men to kill all the young boys two years old and under in Bethlehem and nearby. But after Herod died, an angel of the Lord came to Joseph in a dream while he was in Egypt and told him it was safe to return to the land of the Jews and that he should do so. Joseph obeyed. God told him in a dream to go to the country of Galilee. There, Joseph stayed in a town called Nazareth. It happened just as the early prophets had said: "Jesus will be called a Nazarene."

In every detail of the Christmas story, God was fulfilling His promise to provide the greatest gift of all to the world, the Savior and Messiah, Jesus Christ.

(Adapted from Matthew 2)

Prayers By and About Jesus

As you enjoy the Christmas season this year, think about Jesus in every fun activity. His birth is the reason we celebrate! As you're decorating the house and putting up the tree, think about Jesus—how beautiful and amazing He is! When you're exchanging gifts, think about Jesus—remember all gifts are from Him and in honor of Him. As you're making cookies and candy and enjoying a great big feast, think about Jesus—thank Him for all the yummy food to eat. As you're playing Christmas songs and games, think about Jesus—worship Him for being *Immanuel*, God with us. When you're helping and donating to others, think about Jesus—remember that anything you do for others in need is like serving Jesus Himself. Keep your thoughts on Him, and let all your prayers be filled with knowledge and wonder of Him. The Bible teaches us so much about Jesus, and we learn even from the prayers that He prayed and that others prayed about Him. Read the following stories this month and see for yourself!

"MY EYES HAVE SEEN THE CHOSEN ONE"

Simeon's Prayer About Jesus

An old man named Simeon lived in Jerusalem at the time Jesus was born. Simeon was a good man who loved the one true God and was eagerly looking for the time when God would send the promised Savior to rescue His people. The Holy Spirit had told Simeon that he would not die before he had seen God's Chosen One.

One special day, the Holy Spirit led Simeon to be at the temple. It was the same day Mary and Joseph brought baby Jesus to present Him to God. According to the Jewish law, parents were to give a gift of two young birds on the altar in worship to the Lord.

When Simeon saw baby Jesus at the temple, he was thrilled! God's promise to him had come true. He was finally seeing the Chosen One! Simeon took baby Jesus in his arms. Then he gave honor and thanks to God, saying, "Lord, now let me die in peace, as You have said. My eyes have seen the Chosen One who will save men from the punishment of their sins. You have made Him ready in the sight of all nations. He will be a light to shine on all people."

Joseph and Mary were surprised and wondered about what Simeon had said. Simeon honored and blessed them and said to Mary, the mother of Jesus, "See! This Child will make many people fall and many people rise in the Jewish nation. He will be spoken against and opposed. And a sword will cut through your soul." Simeon was saying that people would either love or reject Jesus, and Mary would be very sad over the way Jesus would be hated by many.

When Joseph and Mary finished what they'd come to do, they left Jerusalem and took baby Jesus back to Nazareth in Galilee. And Jesus grew and became strong in spirit. He was filled with wisdom and the loving-favor of God.

Unlike Simeon, you've never actually seen or touched Jesus. But you know Him through God's Word, the Bible. Pray to know Jesus more and more—someday you *will* see Him face-to-face!

(Adapted from Luke 2:22–40)

"OUR FATHER IN HEAVEN, YOUR NAME IS HOLY"

Jesus' Teaching About How to Pray

Jesus taught in many places while He lived on earth. One day He went up on a mountainside and began to teach about many things to the people who gathered and listened. This was His "Sermon on the Mount." He taught about loving our enemies and giving to the needy. He taught about not worrying and about building up treasure in heaven. He taught about false prophets and a wise builder. He taught about all of that and much more!

Jesus also taught people how to pray. He said, "When you pray, do not be like those people who pretend to be someone they're not. They love to stand and pray where people can see them. Surely, I tell you, they have all the reward they are going to get." He went on, "When you pray, go into a room alone and pray to your Father in secret. Then your Father will reward you. When you pray, do not say the same thing over and over again, making long prayers like the people who do not know God. They think they are heard because their prayers are long. Don't be like them. Your Father knows what you need before you ask Him."

Then Jesus gave us a way to pray. He said, "Pray like this: 'Our Father in heaven, Your name is holy. May Your holy nation come. May what You want done on earth be done as it is in heaven. Give us the bread we need today. Forgive us our sins as we forgive those who sin against us. Do not let us be tempted, but keep us from sin. Your nation is holy. You have power and shining-greatness forever.'"

Jesus didn't mean this is the only prayer we should ever pray. He gave us an example of prayer that we can use to create our own prayers. In all our prayers, we should be sincere and know that God is perfectly holy. We should pray for God's kingdom to come and for His will to be done. We should ask for our daily needs to be met. We should ask for forgiveness for ourselves and for the ability to forgive others. We should ask for help not to sin, and we should praise God. Jesus was so good to teach us this way to pray!

(Adapted from Matthew 6)

"FATHER, HONOR YOUR NAME!"

Jesus' Prayer for God's Glory

Jesus visited His friends Mary, Martha, and Lazarus during the last days before His death on the cross. They made Him supper, and then Mary took a jar of expensive perfume and poured it out on Jesus' feet. Then she dried His feet with her hair. The wonderful smell of the special perfume filled the house. Mary was showing her great love and honor for Jesus.

The next day, many people in Jerusalem heard Jesus was coming, and they were excited to welcome Him. They took palm branches and went to meet Him. They shouted in praise, "Hosanna! Greatest One! Great and honored is He who comes in the name of the Lord, the King of the Jews!" Jesus found a young donkey and sat on it. A prophet named Zechariah had predicted that hundreds of years earlier. He had written, "Do not be afraid, people of Jerusalem. See! Your King comes sitting on a young donkey!"

The people who had been with Jesus when He had called Lazarus from the grave kept telling others about that incredible miracle. They had seen Lazarus raised from the dead! That's why many people wanted to meet Jesus. But the proud religious law keepers were upset that Jesus was there and said among themselves, "Look, we are losing followers. Everyone is following Jesus!"

Jesus said to the people, "The hour is near for the Son of Man to be taken to heaven to receive great honor. Surely, I tell you, unless a seed falls into the ground and dies, it will only be a seed. If it dies, it will give much grain. Anyone who loves their life will lose it. Anyone who hates their life in this world will keep it forever. Anyone who wants to serve Me must follow Me. And My Father will honor anyone who serves Me."

Then Jesus, knowing He would soon suffer and die, said, "Now My soul is troubled. Should I say, 'Father, save Me from this time of trouble and pain'? No, for this is why I came to this time. So, Father, honor Your name!"

Jesus knew God's plan for Him would not be easy. In fact, it would be terrible. But Jesus also knew that God was working out His perfect plan of salvation. Jesus was willing to do whatever His Father told Him. More than anything, Jesus wanted to bring glory to God.

That is our greatest job too. Today, ask God how you can bring Him glory. He'll be happy to answer that prayer.

(Adapted from Zechariah 9; John 12)

"I THANK YOU, FATHER"

Jesus' Prayer of Gratitude

Jesus sent out seventy of His followers, two by two, to the places He would visit and teach in next. He said to them, "There is much grain ready to gather. But the workmen are few. Pray then that the Lord, who owns the grain fields, will send workmen to gather His grain." Jesus meant there were many people who needed to hear about Him and believe.

He said to the followers He sent out, "Go on your way. Listen! I send you out like lambs among wolves. Take no money. Speak to no one along the way. When you go into a house, say that you hope peace will come to them. If your good wishes are not received, they will come back to you."

He continued, "Whenever a city welcomes you, eat the things that are put before you there. Heal the sick. Say to them, 'The holy nation of God is near.' Whatever city does not welcome you, go into its streets and say, 'Know that the holy nation of God has come near you!' I tell you, on the day men stand before God, things will not be easy for that city."

And Jesus said, "Whoever listens to you listens to Me. Whoever has nothing to do with you has nothing to do with Me. Whoever has nothing to do with Me has nothing to do with God, who sent Me."

When the seventy people Jesus had sent out came back, they were full of joy over what Jesus had given them the power to do. They said, "Lord, even the demons obeyed us when we used Your name."

Jesus said to them, "I saw Satan fall from heaven like lightning. Listen! I have given you power to walk on snakes and trample scorpions. I have given you power to defeat the enemy. Nothing will hurt you. Even so, you should not be happy because the demons obey you. Instead, be happy because your names are written in heaven."

And then Jesus was filled with the joy of the Holy Spirit. He said, "I thank You, Father, Lord of heaven and earth. You have shown these things to little children. Yes, Father, it was what You wanted done."

Jesus was grateful to God the Father that eternal life is available to anyone who comes to Him like a little child.

(Adapted from Luke 10)

A YEAR TO CELEBRATE!

New Year's Day

January 1

New Year's Day is the first day of the new year. It's a holiday that helps us look ahead with hope to the coming year.

Martin Luther King Jr. Day

Third Monday in January

Martin Luther King Jr. Day is celebrated near the birthday of Martin Luther King Jr., who was born on January 15, 1929. Martin Luther King Jr. is known and celebrated for his life's work of spreading kindness, fairness, and racial equality among all people.

Valentine's Day

February 14

Valentine's Day is a special day to celebrate and promote love. People give each other cards and gifts and flowers, and many couples celebrate with special dinners too.

Presidents' Day

Third Monday in February

Presidents' Day especially honors two important presidents of the United States of America, George Washington and Abraham Lincoln. It also celebrates all American presidents. It is held near the birthday of the first American president, George Washington, who was born on February 22, 1732.

Saint Patrick's Day

March 17

Saint Patrick's Day is a special day to celebrate Irish traditions because of Saint Patrick, who was a Christian saint remembered and honored for helping to bring Christianity to Ireland.

Ash Wednesday

February or March

Ash Wednesday is the first day of Lent, which is forty days (not including Sundays) of fasting and turning from our sins before the celebration of Easter.

Palm Sunday

The Sunday before Easter

Palm Sunday remembers the day Jesus Christ arrived in Jerusalem on a donkey. The people cut palm branches and laid them in the road for His donkey to walk on while they welcomed and praised Him.

Good Friday

The Friday before Easter

Good Friday remembers the day Jesus Christ was arrested and put to death on the cross to take the punishment for sin and save all who believe in Him.

Easter

A Sunday in March or April

Easter celebrates that Jesus Christ rose to life again after death and that He offers eternal life to all who trust in Him as Savior.

National Day of Prayer

First Thursday in May

The National Day of Prayer is a special day in the United States of America for encouraging people to turn to God in prayer.

Mother's Day

Second Sunday in May

Mother's Day is a special day to remember, honor, and appreciate mothers for their hard work and love in raising their children.

Memorial Day

Last Monday in May

Memorial Day remembers and honors those who have died serving in the military of the United States of America.

Flag Day

June 14

Flag Day remembers when leaders first established a flag to represent the United States of America, during the Revolutionary War, on June 14, 1777.

Father's Day

Third Sunday in June

Father's Day is a special day to remember, honor, and appreciate fathers for their hard work and love in raising their children.

Independence Day

July 4

The Fourth of July honors the day the United States of America declared itself an independent nation and adopted the written Declaration of Independence. Picnics and fireworks are popular ways to celebrate.

Labor Day

First Monday in September

Labor Day is a special day to celebrate American workers.

Veterans Day

November 11

Veterans Day honors all who have served in the armed forces of the United States.

Thanksgiving Day

Fourth Thursday in November

Thanksgiving is a special day to celebrate and give thanks for all things God has given. It's a time for gathering with family and friends and enjoying a feast together.

Christmas Day

December 25

Christmas is the special day to remember and honor the birth of Jesus Christ. People exchange gifts and have many special traditions, foods, and feasts with family and friends to celebrate the season.

MY NOTES

SKETCH PAGE

MY NOTES

SKETCH PAGE

MY NOTES

SKETCH PAGE

MY NOTES

SKETCH PAGE

MY NOTES

SKETCH PAGE